MW01291680

Please See Me. A.L.B.

The Influence of Arthur Lee Burns

Henry Henegar
Jane Henegar
Helen Burns Sharp

Telling Treasures Press
Lookout Mountain, Georgia

ISBN-13: 978-1499333817
ISBN-10: 1499333811

Library of Congress Control Number: 2014910148

Printed by Starkey Printing Company
Chattanooga, TN 37407

PUBLISHED IN THE UNITED STATES OF AMERICA

DEDICATION

Mildred Cooley Burns
1909-1984

"Of course, all the boys and faculty
gave him and Millie
a standing ovation and
everyone yelled and screamed.

"I can still see it."

Larry Gold
McCallie Class of '61

BOY

My father and his brother attended McCallie.
When I decided to attend,
it was drummed into me constantly
to seek out and meet Maj., Major Burns,
as soon as humanly possible. . . .

There he was in a group of boys,
talking and asking questions.
I quickly took a position in a gap.
Maj. noticed, and though he did not know me
he turned and placed his hand on my shoulder.

He said simply "Yes?"

I asked him if he was Major Burns.
He replied, "Yes, and you are?"

I told him my name and he replied
with the most astonishing statement,

"Of course you are!"

His simple statement relayed to me,
"We've been expecting you—
ever since your father graduated."

He was always surrounded by boys.
We all loved and trusted him.

It was like he actually was one of us.

Ed Loughlin '79

CONTENTS

*A teacher's major contribution
may pop out anonymously
in the life of some ex-student's grandchild.*

*A teacher, finally,
has nothing to go on but faith,
a student nothing to offer in return
but testimony.*

Wendell Berry

A man walks down the path of a half-century's familiarity. His back is to our lens, his fedora set resolutely on his graying head, his overcoat broad on a narrowing frame. Underneath that coat is a white shirt that needs no ironing, and a dark tie. Beneath that shirt a strong heart continues its thump-thump, thump-thump.

His bent is not to the weight of sorrows, but to the good weight of worthy years.

It's close to dusk as he traverses the route between the work he loves and the woman he loves: the girl he fell in love with the first moment he saw her. The two poles of his world are an easy distance, and she will be waiting for him at the kitchen table, a pot of coffee on the stove. There will be the day's tales to share, along with the ease of being at home together.

TELLING
what's worth telling

The story of Arthur Lee Burns is a narrow one geographically, almost all of it bounded by a stretch of historic land at the base of a Southern ridge. The first characters in his narrative were grocer John Anderson Burns and his wife Minnie, and his younger siblings Eddie B and Katherine. Then came wife Millie, their son ALB Jr. and daughter Mary Helen, their marriages and seven grandchildren.

Now begins a parade of thousands into ALB's story, names and faces he well remembered, on the grounds of The McCallie School, an independent day and boarding school for boys. Arthur Lee Burns became a schoolman. The three-mile limit of most of his daily steps from birth to death--the small physical scale of his life--belies the breadth and beauty of his reach. The stories that define ALB are magnets, drawing back those who grew up under his care. They might as well draw any man or woman in any place: This is what it looks like to live among those who love you enough to talk to you straight, not to give up on you, and to laugh long all along.

Something happens when you become a teacher, a committed teacher living out your gifts in the life of a school. Your students' definition of family, heretofore narrow, begins to push the margins. Your arms open wider too.

Some things happened in the life of ALB that became part of many stories of many boys, and their many families. After all, despite the goodness of one's own origins, where would any child be without other adults to become heroes, confidants, trainers, challengers and allies? And friends.

And despite the heartaches of one's own origins, what troubles cannot be lightened with somebody like Major Burns walking beside you, arm on your shoulder?

However.

There was only one Arthur Lee Burns.

As the years pass without diminution of his influence, those who carried a scrap of ALB into the person they would become have kept telling his stories. They have written letters, have gathered around his memory at home and abroad. In the retelling they laughed again and cried again. These gathered scraps, these legends and these rooting truths became a telling treasure. Their stories woven into his story insist on being told.

Sometimes his boys waxed poetic, as did Rob Betz in these lines describing his teacher as "a man, not a founder, or even a member of a founding family, just a man who ate the bread he worked for, did the job he was paid for, and every decade bought a new suit."

There was an evening when Burns, a French teacher, stood beside his daughter's desk as she puzzled over her math homework. "Once, I almost understood logarithms," was all he could offer.

"There were a lot of things my father almost understood," that daughter remembers. "But he well understood everything that matters."

To help the reader understand, consider one boy in the late 1940s. His name was Jimmy Williams, and he was a day student from North Georgia. "I rode the public bus or hitch-hiked to get to and from school every day. One morning my bus broke down and I was several miles away. I got several short rides and ran the last mile, trying to get to school on time and avoid the demerit.

"As I ran up the steps to chapel I heard the student body singing 'Love Lifted Me.'

"I knew I was late and after chapel went straight to Major Burns' office as required. I expected the worst and knew I would pay a dear price for my tardiness. When I told Major

Burns why I was late he stood up, walked around his desk, put his arm around me and told me he was surprised I got here as soon as I did. He complimented me on how hard I tried to be on time and told me there would be no penalty."

Young Williams continued to expend every last burst of energy to get where he needed to be, becoming corporate chairman of SunTrust Bank in Atlanta. How does a boy who has to run to catch up learn to lead like that? He pays attention to a day like this one. "Major taught me a lot about leadership and about life during those few minutes. Before, I had admired him and even feared him. But after that I loved and respected him."

And though these lessons might just as easily be delivered in bursts of eraser-throwing anger as by gentle instruction, his students, his boys, understood them well. The wisest among those boys continue to live by them.

Today we say, let's pass them on.

ALB
initially

The McCallie School is nestled at the foot of Missionary Ridge in Chattanooga, Tenn., along the site of the 1863 Civil War Battle of Missionary Ridge. Once the 40-acre McCallie family farm, this narrow stretch of land has served as academic home to thousands of lively boys since 1905.

Carved in stone at the entrance are the school's guiding words from the Westminster Catechism: "Man's Chief End is to Glorify God and Enjoy Him Forever."

Other words, engraved on the minds and hearts of boys who would become men, have been chiseled by both delight and difficulty inside these gates. But in the long history of the school, perhaps no other words have been more telling than the ones that follow, always written in a precise and graceful vertical script, always on a scrap of reclaimed paper, such as the back of a discarded student roster:

please see me ALB

Countless such notes came into the hands of boys in the 52 years on campus of ALB, Arthur Lee Burns Sr., known early on as Bud and forever after as Major Burns or Maj. He began as a teacher and made his mark as dean of students and associate headmaster until his 1972 retirement at the obligatory 70. This terse summons--"Please see me"--from Maj. could fill a boy with terror and cause him to rummage frantically through his conscience for all recent sins and infractions. It could compel him to pull down his shirtsleeves, pull up his tie, and then check his breath for telltale evidence of cigarette smoke.

A summons to the dean's office could also fill him with hope, because up until the delivery of that note, the boy might not have mattered to much of anybody, might have sorely needed noticing. Uncannily, as former head Spencer McCallie III saw, Maj. could tell who needed him, and just what was needed.

Fear and hope, as they are wont to do, often worked together to get a boy through Major Burns' office door. His desk in old North Hall faced the wall, so the boy might first be recipient of Maj.'s. solemn over-the-shoulder scrutiny. Whatever happened next, it was bound to fit the boy.

Senator Howard H. Baker Jr., McCallie Class of 1943, wrote, "In all my travels, many people have made a lasting impression on me. However, in my youth...none have compared with you."

His colleagues, his fellow teachers, were also watching and learning. In his mind's eye teacher Jim Lyle still sees Maj. "with 7,231 scraps of paper in his hands. He is looking over the top of his glasses with those huge brown eyes and reading infinite lists of boys who must do something, didn't do something, or must go see somebody.

"Maj. must have averaged two hours sleep each day. He was the last person seen on campus each night and the first every morning."

We see you still, ALB.

MILLIE
lightened him up

George K. Brown's Palace, an ice cream emporium, was the center of a small universe in the days of Prohibition in downtown Chattanooga, Tenn.

Ice cream was one of the few legal indulgences in those days, and Brown's gleaming mahogany and marble shop drew young people from all over town.

The streetcar route stopped at the corner of 7th and Market, a busy intersection. Businessmen hurried to their tasks; mothers pushed their little ones in canvas-covered strollers. And on any warm afternoon, students fled for an ice cream cone or soda to Brown's lavishly decorated Palace.

On a fall day in 1927 a tall, wavy-haired young teacher took a break from his duties at McCallie School a few miles east of downtown. This was the school from which he had graduated seven years earlier, the school he returned to as a teacher as soon as he graduated from Emory University, bearing into the classroom his Master's degree.

Now a veteran of two years teaching, and already part of the fabric of the school still led by its founders, the brothers McCallie, Burns had reached his 25th birthday. And in the autumn sunshine, in the company of another teacher, he headed down McCallie Avenue. They might have traveled by streetcar, but chances are good Burns was driving his first vehicle, a Chevrolet coupe. The Depression, however, was looming, and soon the streetcar would be his only means of travel to town.

On spring days in later years he would caution boys, as they headed to town in hopes of meeting girls, "Sap's rising, boys. Sap's rising."

But on this day he heeded no caution, stepping out on Market Street and looking toward the Palace entrance where a young woman stood with a friend. A brown-haired, brown-eyed girl, lively and laughing, she was wearing the pastel linen uniform of her school, GPS, (the private Girls Preparatory School).

She was 18.

He caught his breath as she turned and entered the store, and then found himself wordlessly following her. The ceiling fans were whirring and the long white-tiled room was noisy with conversation. As she stood at the counter ordering her usual single-dip butter pecan cone, the young teacher pulled a McCallie student aside.

"Who is that girl?"

"Sir, that is Millie Cooley," the boy answered respectfully.

Burns responded, but only to himself: "That is the girl I want to marry."

Young Burns acted on his initial inclination, finding a McCallie student to make the introductions. The following July, not long after her 19th birthday, he eloped with Millie to nearby Cleveland, Tenn. For a few days they kept the secret, planning to wait to tell family and friends until ALB returned from Army summer camp at Fort McClellan, Ala. But Millie told her pastor, who advised her that, "If you married him, you are to live together." So she told her parents, who sat on the porch and cried all night. Then they ordered the proper formal announcements of the marriage.

One of those announcements arrived at the campus home of school founder Dr. Park McCallie, widely admired and often feared for his unyielding moral rectitude. You might imagine the effect of this news: a teacher eloping with a student in the tight Chattanooga community of long ago. Dr. McCallie wrote back immediately, on the school letterhead.

Think of his loyal employee, the bridegroom,

opening the missive with trepidation. It began "Dear Arthur Lee," continued with congratulations, including this line: "She must be a fine girl if you chose her," and ended with a handwritten, light-hearted chiding. "I am mad at you for not inviting me to your wedding."

Whew.

No wonder he kept that note always. Its graciousness may be early evidence that the McCallie family placed implicit trust in the judgment of ALB. That well-founded trust never wavered.

Martha Smallwood was a freshman at GPS when she came home from summer camp to hear that Millie Cooley had married a McCallie teacher. "We all loved her, because she was so much fun and was nice even to us younger girls." she recollected near her own 101st birthday. "We all thought it was the most romantic thing. Our parents were worried anyway, but of course this made them worry even more. Nobody talked about the marriage except the adults. We weren't allowed. But for the next few years, whenever families got together, if there were young girls in the family one of the parents would always say, 'Now girls, be sure you don't get married before you are ready.' "

Martha Smallwood listened, despite the romance she and her classmates had witnessed with longing. When she was an ancient 22 years old, she married another McCallie graduate and future teacher, Harry "Sack" Milligan.

On the Cooleys' end, they couldn't have grieved long, said Martha. "After all, Arthur Lee had a **job**."

Millie moved with her husband into a house at 1201 Duncan Avenue, thus forfeiting her senior year at GPS. A year later the departure of Wendell Wren from the faculty made an apartment in Douglas Hall available. "The basis of rental will be $35.00 a month," Dr. McCallie wrote, "which will include lights, water, heat, and gas. You will furnish your own furniture." Imagine that: ALB had to pay to live over the boiler room!

Nine years after their elopement they produced Arthur's namesake, and almost a decade after that came Mary Helen.

It would be less than accurate to say the Burnses lived a charmed life; 23 years of it were spent in the small apartment above said boiler room. As the 1940s turned to the 1950s, often the boiler's safety valve would go off and Maj.'s job was to usher everybody safely out onto Kyle Street—his family and the students. Finally someone in town heard about the need, was horrified and paid for the repairs.

Still, the honeymoon wasn't over. "Some of our happiest years," Millie believed, "were when we had the least money. We used to walk down to the streetcar to ride into town for an ice cream cone (called 'a horn of cream' at Kay's Ice Cream Shop in those days) and the motorman would stop for us in the middle of the block.

"When we married, I could picture us sitting in front of the fire, Maj. smoking a pipe with a Collie dog at his feet." There never was pipe or Collie, or even much sitting, but she confirmed that "it's been a wonderful life. I can't think of anybody I would rather be married to." One day Maj. opened his mouth to call his bride the usual "Honey" and it just came out "Huggie." That term of endearment stuck. The marriage lasted 49 years, until his death.

The children had the utmost respect and affection for their mother. She welcomed boys into her home in the dormitory until 1956 when they moved into a faculty house on Kyle Street. It was sometimes a tough row to hoe, and nobody doubts that Millie was responsible for much of Maj.'s success. Their home was open to the boys, and when they graduated and wrote Maj., these fellows inquired about Mrs. Burns, little Bud, and little Mary Helen. Mrs. Burns was willing to be submerged in the McCallie culture, and Bud's wife Graham confirms that "her willingness was a big part of his success."

Maj.'s sister Katherine said of her own family, "The Burnses were a little stuffy," but said this of her sister-in-law: "Millie was anything but stuffy. Millie was his salvation; she lightened him up." Their daughter said, "It would be hard to over-state her contributions to his happiness. His world became their world. She never complained, even though the campus environment during that era could be considered a little confining for someone with her personality and *joie de vivre*."

CHILDREN
one of each

Despite almost a decade's age difference (son born in 1937, daughter in 1946), Maj. and Millie's children stayed close.

Arthur Lee Jr. chose to be called Bud when he went off to Emory University, just as his father had done before him. Mary Helen shortened herself to Helen in elementary school. Bud was a college senior and Helen a seventh grader when big brother offered her the invitation of her young lifetime: "Come spend the weekend with me at Emory." What an evidence of brotherly love!

Helen rode the bus to Atlanta and Bud borrowed a friend's car to meet her. He arranged for her to stay with a friend in a girls' dormitory. He took her to movies at the Fox and Loew's Grand, and to a basketball game at Georgia Tech, and introduced her to a trendy new food: pizza. Helen came home "probably insufferable," having acquired a new college vocabulary that included describing movies as flicks.

Both children roamed free in the idyllic childhood world of the school campus. Home was first an apartment in old Douglas Hall (until 1952); then an apartment in South Hutcheson Hall (until 1956), and finally in a two-story house at 710 Kyle Street.

Every morning Maj. was the family breakfast cook, frying bacon in a cast iron skillet and then frying the eggs in the bacon drippings. Brother and sister were in college before learning that the egg white was supposed to be white and that the unsullied yolk belongs in the center of a fried egg.

They played with other faculty children, and swam at McCallie Lake, where Bud was bold enough to jump or dive off the iron steps. They walked, took the streetcar (Bud) or carpooled (Helen) to Missionary Ridge Elementary School. They went to the junction on Dodds Avenue to get ice cream cones at Kay's. On Saturdays they sometimes saw movies at the Brainerd Theater. Best of all, they could drop in to see their father in the O.D. Room in North Hall.

Young Bud attended McCallie camp in the summers. Faculty sons could attend school free or at a greatly reduced rate, so he went to McCallie for grades 7 through 12, making the very short walk from Douglas or South Hutch to the academic building. Camp for Helen was out of the question on a tight teacher's salary. The year she rode the bus to Emory to meet Bud, Helen received a scholarship to a new world--a school for girls--her mother's alma mater, GPS. (Located across town on the north shore of the Tennessee River, Girls Preparatory School was founded a year after McCallie, and one of the founders was the McCallie founders' sister Grace.)

Financial limitations were many, but satisfactions provided a balance. Helen once overheard her parents discussing whether to pay Miller Brothers or Loveman's that month: they couldn't pay the entire bill for both downtown department stores. The family had meat once a week and Cokes on special occasions. Milk was only for the children. Neither parents nor children complained; it was their financial reality. In the balance, Maj.'s job satisfaction, the children's educational opportunities and the campus community mitigated the lack of disposable income.

The children made popcorn and listened to the St. Louis Cardinals on radio KMOX. Bud and his parents and friends listened to radio shows. Neighbor Richard Park and Bud particularly enjoyed westerns and "Baby Snooks." In 1952 television came to Chattanooga and Helen and her father took to watching "What's My Line?" and "Gunsmoke" together. One night the family was watching "The Perry Como Show," sponsored by Kraft. The commercials for cheese sandwiches were not appealing to Helen, as she told her father, "because the mayonnaise oozes off the sides of the bread.' Maj. changed her perspective by explaining, "The messier something looks, the better it tastes." This Burnsian principle could be applied to the daily egg scramble, darkened with bacon drippings in that iron skillet. Perhaps it also applies to making the most, every day, of what might be a limited or even scrambled bill of fare.

The Major Burns temper, famous among the boys, also manifested itself with his family from time to time. It happened when Maj. taught Helen to drive. "I don't know whom this was harder on, father or daughter. We went to Warner Park for my lessons. By the time we got home, I was in tears and he was mad, not so much at me as at himself for not being able to get through to me. I remember telling my mother that I never wanted to be in a car with him again.

"Maj. wasn't a particularly good driver, but he excelled at parallel parking. Somehow, he was able to pass this skill on to me. To this day I almost seek opportunities for parallel parking and I think about my father every time."

Neither child learned much about home repair from their father; time and inclination were lacking. Bud's good friend Richard Park recounts: "Maj., with all his qualities, was not a handyman. Their home on Kyle Street was adjacent to our home. In contrast to Maj., my dad seemed to have some magical ability to fix almost anything. I recall a number of occasions that my father was called to the Burns home to stop the leak or whatever." Maj. had to stoke the coal-fired furnace in the basement of their Kyle

Street home. For Helen, living over the family furnace was about as scary as living over the boiler room in Douglas Hall.

Given the perception that he worked 24/7, people sometimes asked the Burns children if he were ever at home. Helen says, "The short answer is yes. In fact, I may have had more interaction with my father on a daily basis than many of my classmates had with theirs. When he was home, he was home, although the telephone did ring a lot, with boys calling to check in. Given the proximity of home and office, it was akin to living above the store."

Maj. and Millie came to visit when Helen was in graduate school at the University of Texas. "I was thrilled but a little concerned about what they would think, since UT Austin was one of the most liberal college campuses in the county during the Viet Nam era. My most vivid memory of their visit involves our stroll across campus in the vicinity of the famous Texas Tower. Hundreds of students were headed for classes, dressed in everything imaginable. Maj. wore a coat and tie, of course. As we walked, a young man with hair below his waist and no shirt stopped Maj., shook his hand, and said: 'How are you today, sir?' "

We know the respect that McCallie boys had for him on a small campus over 900 miles away and we understand why. They knew him and knew what he stood for. But what made this young stranger take that initiative and pay his respects?

What was it about ALB at first glance that revealed the man within?

* * *

Maj. admitted, and it is recorded within these covers, his tenderness for and also enjoyment of the boys who got themselves into a little trouble.

It happened with his girl, too.

"During graduate school I was home from Austin for the summer and worked at *The Chattanooga Times*. One evening after work, I went with friends to get a bite to eat. Actually, we did a bit more drinking than eating that night. I got home about midnight. While I didn't have to check out, I certainly should have called my parents and told them where I was and when I would be home. I remember pulling in the driveway, hoping so much that they would be in bed asleep. (Many a McCallie boy can sympathize here.)

"Maj., of course, greeted me at the door. He said: 'Hi, honey. It's late. Get some sleep. Tomorrow is a work day.' That, of course, made me feel even worse because I knew I had worried them unnecessarily and he was being so dadgum gracious about it.

"The next morning I still felt bad. In addition to the well-deserved hangover, I felt like I had let my parents down. Maj. must have sensed my angst. At lunchtime, I went to the break room to try to eat the sandwich and apple he had packed for me in a brown bag. When I reached into the bag, I found this note. On a piece of recycled paper he had written: 'I love you Daddy.' "

Helen married Corry Sharp in 1977, shortly after her father's death, and in 1990 they left Tennessee for Oregon. When Corry died of cancer in 2001, Bud was there to shore Helen up. After retirement Helen bought a condominium overlooking the Tennessee River in downtown Chattanooga. She was looking forward to spending more time with brother Bud and his family, as well as seeing more of her stepchildren and grandchildren. Unfortunately, Bud died unexpectedly in 2008 after back surgery.

As this book took shape the sister took up her pen (her keyboard) on her brother's behalf, remembering childhood for them both. She knew well that Bud's affection and respect for ALB were enormous. "Oftentimes he would tear up when our father's name was mentioned."

Jim Daughdrill Jr. wrote Bud Jr. after ALB's death. "You said of your father that 'He was the finest person I ever met.' I agree. But to have your own son say that about you must be life's biggest moment." His words form a kind of benediction to this chapter, telling what it meant to be Maj.'s own children.

Bud Burns Jr. and Helen Burns Sharp
in Grants Pass, Oregon, 2000

WHENCE
general and major issues

The ingredients in ALB's ancestry were Scottish, Irish and English, with a twist of German and Swiss. Did he know and understand his family's defining names and places? This much is clear. Maj. was a man who lived in the present, but he would surely read his lineage with appreciation, assuming and expecting (as he always did) the best from everyone.

Branches on the Burns side include Rapers and Lewises. On his mother's side, the names include Huffakers, Riggenses, and Eppersons.

His European ancestors crossed the pond before the Declaration of Independence in 1776--adventurers all.

In their road trips to Tennessee--all arrived before statehood in 1796--they likely traveled along the Great Valley/Philadelphia Wagon Road. The road began in Philadelphia. It split in

Big Lick, Va. (now Roanoke). One fork went through Virginia to Knoxville, Tenn. The other fork continued through Virginia into North Carolina before ending in Augusta, Ga.

Long before they merged in the lineage of ALB, we can imagine that those ancestral settlers in their wagons crossed paths at one of the all-important forks in the road.

ALB's fifth great grandfather may have been General Andrew Lewis, a brigadier general in the Revolutionary War, friend of Washington and Jefferson. A statue of General Lewis is among those honoring Virginia patriots on the Washington monument in Richmond's capital square. Lewisburg, W.Va. is named for him, as is a portion of Interstate 81 near Roanoke, Va.

What would the General think of his descendant, the perennial Major?

NEST
East Chattanooga

John Anderson Burns and Minnie Huffaker Burns became parents on July 26, 1902. Both had moved to Chattanooga with their families about 1890, he from Polk County, Tenn. (Benton) and she from Whitfield County, Ga. (Cohutta). His mother had a brother named Arthur. His father had a brother named Lee. Hence, their firstborn was called Arthur Lee.

John owned a grocery store on Glass Street in East Chattanooga from about 1905 until 1932. (The store was a casualty of the Great Depression--many customers could no longer pay their bills.) Unlike his son, who was lanky and brown-eyed and studious, he was short, had gray eyes, was spontaneous and loved being outdoors. He was always ready for a picnic or a visit to see relatives in McDonald, Tenn. or an outing on Chickamauga Creek.

Minnie was a seamstress at the pants factory in East Chattanooga until her marriage in 1901.

Her great niece Virginia Stanfiel Wrinkle remembers that Minnie cooked a mean skillet of fried corn. She was a tall woman with dark brown eyes, two characteristics she shared with her oldest child (the younger two favored their father).

ALB was close to his mother. She died in 1936 when he was 34, having passed her innate kindness on to her boy. During ALB's childhood the family lived at 3302 North Chamberlain Avenue and then on Taylor Street, where he and his brother slept on the sleeping porch. Both houses were close to the grocery store on Glass Street. The Burnses attended King Memorial Methodist Church, located a few blocks south of the Taylor Street house. (Arthur Lee was a lifelong Methodist, even attending Methodist-affiliated Emory University.) Tige was the Burns family dog. When he wasn't at home on Taylor Street, Tige was "working" at the grocery store.

His brother Eddie B (the B didn't stand for anything) was born two years to the day after ALB. Eddie B went to McCallie for a period but decided that Central High School would be more fun. He became a fireman, rising to the rank of Assistant Chief. An engine bore his name. He rode such an engine out to McCallie School as first responder when a dormitory, Jarnagin Hall, burned in 1952. An alumni magazine article has a picture of Capt. Eddie Burns sitting on the steps recovering from smoke, watched over by his big brother Arthur.

Sister Katherine did not arrive until 1918; this was not a family that rushed things. By the time she was old enough for secondary school, the Depression was in full swing, so private school and college were not options. She went to Chattanooga High School and to McKenzie Business School. She soloed at the Chattanooga Airport in 1940 at the age of 22, worked as a legal secretary for several prominent law firms in Chattanooga and then as an abstractor for the Tennessee Valley Authority. Katherine and their father John Burns shared a home until his death in 1958 at the age of 83.

In 1936 a high school classmate asked her to marry him. The answer had to wait 34 years. (Again, no hurry.) She said "Yes" at age 52. Was marriage worth the wait? Katherine said she liked being married so much she wished she had married at 50.

While both Eddie B and Katherine married, neither had children. ALB's wife Millie was an only child. So the two Burns children, Arthur Jr. and Helen, had no first cousins. Since they grew up in faculty housing on the McCallie campus, other faculty children served as surrogate cousins, or as Jim McCallie notes elsewhere, sometimes like siblings.

The McCallie School
Missionary Ridge
Chattanooga, Tennessee

August 16, 1928

Mr. Arthur Lee Burns,

East Chattanooga, Tennessee.

Dear Arthur Lee:

I have just received the announcement of your marriage with Miss Cooley. To say that I was surprised to hear that you were married is expressing it mildly. I thought you were a confirmed "old bachelor" and did not know that any of the girls had sat their caps for you. In fact I had become quite convinced that you were immune but it shows how poor our judgement is. I know you must have gotten a nice girl for you would not have any other kind. I wish for you and her the happiest possible married life.

With best wishes,

Yours sincerely,

J. P. McCallie, Headmaster,

JPMcC-GH

P.S. I am mad at you for not inviting me to the wedding

J. P. McCallie to ALB:
"I thought you were a 'confirmed old bachelor.'"

28

SCHOLAR
prized

As the 20th century dawned, Miss Ella Heaton opened a private school in her home in East Chattanooga. It was a few blocks' walk from the Burns home, and Miss Heaton was the logical one for John and Minnie to entrust with their firstborn from first through seventh grade. Burns family lore has it that he was her prize student, and that Miss Heaton urged his parents to give Arthur a chance at McCallie.

John Burns knew Professor S. J. McCallie, one of the school's founders, having worked with him on community projects. His parents wanted Arthur to continue to get the best education possible and the new McCallie School, founded in 1905, filled that bill. Apparently he could not enter McCallie before his freshman year (1916), so he spent the eighth grade at East Chattanooga Elementary School.

Young Arthur's years as a student at McCallie spanned 1916 to 1920, which coincidentally included America's time in World War I. The 1920 *Pennant*, the school yearbook, described him as a strong supporter of the honor system. "He is quiet and manly in bearing and commands the respect of all who know him." Hornsby Wasson was two years behind Burns, and remembers one day when the two were walking with a teacher on campus. "For some unknown reason I picked up a rock and threw it against the building nearby. The faculty member promptly gave me my first demerit ever. I was distraught and Arthur came over to me and put his arm on my shoulder and said something like this: 'Don't feel too bad. There are plenty of rocks and wild onions to pick up around here and you can work off those demerits in no time.' "

So the hand on the shoulder was an early trademark. For Wasson, later it was the same hand proffered at a gas pump. "I ran a service station in East Chattanooga one summer. Arthur was one of my regular visitors and if more help was needed on occasion he would pitch in as if he were an employee."

As was the student, so was the man. What makes a youthful honor endure into adulthood? How crucial is the presence of someone older, walking alongside, comforting and pitching in to get the work done?

What made the man ALB?

Would Burns have become who he was if Professor McCallie hadn't seen his potential as a teacher and suggested, in his senior year at McCallie, that after Emory he come back to teach? Would he have become the one Hornsby Wasson described as "a deeply religious person, seeing good in all of us," if others hadn't first seen and spoken of the good in him? Watch for clues to those answers.

Burns earned his Bachelor of Arts and Master of Arts degrees at Emory University (1920-1925) with a major in French. He enjoyed college life in Atlanta. As a prelude to his later military title, he was a First Lieutenant in the Reserve Officers Training Corps. In his senior year, he was in charge of the freshman dormitory. Among his first boys was Bob Ware, who would marry Professor Spencer McCallie's daughter Mary.

Another boy was Prentice Miller, Emory class of 1927, who remembered a half-century later that Arthur was his proctor in Room 316--"the only room number I remember in my years in the dormitories. I was very, very fond of him."

When he was home from Emory in the summers, Burns helped out at his father's grocery store. As a college man, his assignment was to help with bookkeeping. Each summer he spent time at Lake Junaluska, N.C. where he worked as a waiter in the old Terrace Hotel at the Methodist conference center.

After joining the faculty at McCallie, ALB studied French the summer of 1945 at Middlebury College in Vermont. And so ended his student days, unless you count his constant studiousness in knowing boys.

BOY
called you boy
but knew your name

ALB. MAJ. BOY: The definitive three-letter terms of this account.

A new student arrived at school and when Burns greeted him, he called him Boy. After that introduction ALB would never again forget his name. And he would keep calling him Boy, even into adulthood.

Decades after graduation, Bill Lorino often came back to see his mentor, who had "endured my failures with enough faith in me to make me better...and shared in the success of all of us with sufficient humility to compensate for our pride."

The signature on Lorino's note to Maj., announcing his visit in an easily recognizable hand, was simply: BOY

Here is the first Maj. paradox. You were always Boy, but from the moment of your meeting, he knew and kept on knowing your name. And your hometown.

Jim (Pogo) Maddox writes: "In the mid 1970s I had the opportunity to show McCallie to our young children and I was able to introduce them to Maj.—a special occasion. I will always remember his question to our oldest son, age seven at the time:

" 'What's your name, Boy?'

"Among many noble traits was Maj.'s consistency."

***

In February of their senior year, Bob Walker and Phil Whitley checked out to Lookout Mountain to visit some female acquaintances. While they were walking with them around the east brow, it began to snow. The beauty of it all added a romantic fever to the afternoon--which intensified as the snow continued to fall. It was suggested that it might be <u>very</u> dangerous for the two of them to try to get back to school that afternoon, and that the most prudent and safe course would be for them to suffer some class absences and to stay on the mountain for the night. They hoped of course that the elements might let up and free them sometime later in the week.

"We stopped to use the pay phone at the Incline Railway station," Walker writes. "We wanted to call Maj. and tell him we were stranded and not to worry about us--as we knew he would. I got him on the phone and laid out our very difficult circumstance, obviously beyond our control--including how much we hated to miss Mr. Chism's English class on Monday.

"There was a long silence--then he said:

" 'What is that noise, Boy (as only he could say the word Boy)?'

" 'What noise?' says I.

" 'That screeching noise.'

" 'Oh, that! I think that must be the Incline, Maj.'

"Silence. Then: 'Ride that Incline, Boy (as only he could say Boy), Ride that Incline.'

" 'But Maj., it's so steep. It's screeching, probably bad brakes. Phil is scared of heights.'

" 'Ride that incline, Boy, ride that incline!' CLICK.

"We were present in Mr. Chism's class on Monday morning."

***

The younger Burns child was born 18 years after her parents' marriage. In her childhood they lived in Douglas Hall, built in 1907 as the first dormitory on campus. Little Helen liked to look out the window at the land now occupied by Spears Stadium, then only an athletic field but also where McCallie students would do military drills and walk the bullring to work off their marks.

One morning toddler Helen turned from the window to her parents, pointed across to the field filled with students, and spoke her first word:

"BOY!"

"I saw a lot of boys," she confirmed. "I also heard my father use the word a time or two."

NAMES
yours, your father's and your brother's

David Balloff stayed on the straight and narrow at McCallie for a simple reason: "Everyone in my family went to McCallie and Major Burns knew them all. I was always too scared to go over the line. Sometimes he called me Sam and sometimes Mark." Did he confuse his Balloffs, or was he simply reminding himself--and them--who the current Balloff belonged to? We favor the latter answer.

The family name could have another effect, as it did for Tom Makepeace, whose father's McCallie days ended "after a year of sneaking out of the dormitory for hamburgers on Dodds Avenue, among other things. For my first six months as a McCallie student, Maj. called me Jimmy and I kept thinking that I had to live down my father's reputation. Major Burns never forgot his boys or the details of their time at McCallie."

The Striblings, Charles the elder and younger,

visited campus together in 1966. Father had graduated in the illustrious class of '42 and was bringing his son to Academic Enrichment Camp. Much had changed, but the father began the tour by turning toward Maj.'s office and saying, "Son, there is somebody I'd like you to meet."

Here son picks up the story. "We walked into Maj.'s office and this tall, gray-haired man looked up and said, 'Hello Charles. Hello Charles Jr.' I realized then that this was a man endowed with special powers. What a way to be intro-duced to McCallie."

The name McGregor appears often in the Burns family boxes of letters. The usual postmark: Managua, Nicaragua. From 3000 miles away the McGregors sent Chico ('48), Pancho ('52), Alberto ('55), Don ('78), Adolfo ('79), and Alberto ('82), and in the next generation Ryan and William and John McGregor. In the earlier days, the post office was the conduit for almost all communication.

From home came packages for the boys. Don, who arrived from Managua at age 13, was checking his mailbox and found the famous little piece of paper with Please See Me. ALB.

"When I found him at the O.D. Room he said, 'Donald, it appears that Chico and your mother remembered your birthday,' and handed me a brown box that had come in the mail. Then, 'Make sure you share those goodies with your friends at the dormitory.'

"Maj. took every single opportunity to teach us a positive value one way or another. He is definitely one of the greatest influences in my life. The very first time in my life that I cried at a funeral was at his, when I had the great honor to be chosen as part of the honor guard for Maj.'s body."

***

There were complications when there was a surfeit of one name, as logically happened to a Smith. George Blackwell Smith III found a solution and Maj. went along. Smith got the Please See Me note and was relieved that it was only to select a distinguishing initial for his school nametag.

"My first suggestion was the double initial G.B. This would create an unacceptable alphabetical issue and we needed just one initial different from all other Smiths. Then a great idea struck me: X! I could be Smith, X. This was great for me, certainly in keeping with the spirit of the 1960s. Sort of radical; Malcolm X, Smith, X. I loved it.

"I'll never forget the look of surprise over the glasses riding low on his nose. He repeated it slowly, 'Smith (pause) X.' 'Yes Sir,' I asserted, 'Smith, X.' 'We are quite sure about this?' he asked, with a hint of a smile on his face, pencil poised to make the decisive mark. He repeated, 'Smith, X.' 'Yes Sir, Maj. Smith, X.' And with that he marked it down with a look of amusement.

"Our appointment ended with, 'That is all, thank you, Smith, X.' "

You might have been the lone member of your family at McCallie, and your name too stuck with the Major. Wiley Adkins brought his wife to see the school a decade after graduation. "It was early in the evening, probably around seven. We went inside to look around and saw a light on in the O.D. Room. Sitting at the desk was Maj. He looked up and said, "Hello Wiley, how have you been?"

Just like that, a decade erased, a conversation resumed seamlessly though the boy had become a husband.

FATHER
perennial substitute

He was father, but also grandfather. And mother, and enduringly, patriarch.

In a letter to son Bud, an alumnus described him also as a miracle, in that "almost every student experienced this feeling of his care. I suppose it was easy for him to care for the 'good' boys but he showed that same caring to those who spent so much time with the Discipline Committee and on the bullring. Even the 'dog boys' [seniors who had never risen above the rank of private] knew and sensed that love."

Now THERE is a hint for the best possible fathering, mothering, or teaching: unconditional caring.

Why would this writer ask to remain anonymous? Possibly for this reason. His final sentence was, "No one had more influence on my life, not even my own parents during those years, than your father."

In truth there is nothing disloyal in the alumnus's words here, only respect for his parents. The ones who conceived us find it near-impossible to distance themselves from us. Parental figures outside the family, however, help us to see ourselves as individuals and to grow into our own unique selves instead of an admired parent's clone.

Robert Sims marveled at "the time he spent with our problems, the hopes he had for our future! If I had a second father, I would have wanted him to be Bud [ALB]."

In senior English the boys studied Victor Hugo's *Les Miserables*. It was perhaps startling that every year they recognized Maj. in an unlikely character: Inspector Javert. Their teacher, Spencer McCallie III, thinks it makes perfect sense, though his younger brother Franklin objects to the parallel of the mean Javert with the anything-but-mean Maj.

Older brother made his point. 'Every year they saw that Maj. was Javert. Javert never gives up. You learn you cannot escape. You cannot just ignore him. He's the main man." There the similarity ends, and here Maj. becomes a quite different inspector. "He's grandfather and he's dad and you are not going to just slough it off. You have got to see the man, no matter what you did [with your own father] at home.

"If you want to find the boys who are in trouble, find the boys who have tardies and absences and are avoiding you. Then you become the chief counselor by finding the boys who are in trouble. Maj. was mining the data; he had the notes of the boys who didn't come in on time. There were no loose ends; he tied up the loose ends. But that's only half of it.

"He is trying to find out who needs him."

Trying to find out who needs him: this may be the *modus operandi* that led Maj. all the way.

His watchfulness, like a father's, did not ignore the business at hand. In the 1940s three alumni, then students at Harvard, were discussing ALB over dinner. Howard Cannon said, "Yes I think Mr. Burns was the first person whom I liked there. He was the first to be friendly. He came over and talked with me once when I was homesick--and then told me to get a haircut."

It happened often in the 52 McCallie years that a second generation of one family saw Maj. as a father, therefore making him a kind of wise grandfather, too. One such family was the Talley family of Knoxville. The patriarch, Jim, was in the legendary class of 1942 that sent many members off to war. His son Jay, also a boarding student, here weaves the familial threads.

"During my freshman year, which is very tentative, I was homesick a lot. Toward the end of Christmas break, I came down with the flu. I returned several days late and was over-whelmed with the amount of homework that had accumulated due to the classes I had missed. I called my father and told him that I could not catch up. He told me that he would come back to Chattanooga the next day and take me home. After getting off the phone with me, he called Major Burns. Dad looked up to Major Burns as a father, since his own father died when Dad was only three. Maj. told Dad that he had the situation under control and that he would work things out with me. He then came down to Douglas Hall and had a heart-to-heart talk with me. He told me that things were not as hopeless as they seemed and that he would make sure I caught up.

"Four years later I graduated from McCallie. I owe this all to the talk Maj. had with me during my freshman year."

An alumnus mused aloud to the Burns family, "I've wondered how it must have felt to share your father with so many of us. So many, especially boarding students, considered ourselves his boys."

No musing necessary from the other end. Home for the Burns family was a dormitory apartment, and later a two-story home on campus. Whatever the building, home was entirely home. "He kept long hours, yes. But he was home, too." Helen affirms that "he never shortchanged us." When Helen was sick, he was downright mad that he couldn't make her well. He followed the careers of each child with gusto and was well on his way to doing the same with his first five grandchildren. Their mother Graham likes to imagine the fun he would have had watching their athletic exploits. He was, after all, coach of the Mid-South Champion tennis team in the early 1940s. And his grandchildren's sport of choice was almost always tennis.

Is this not a crucial part of an examination of the man's character, that he first met his primary responsibility, his own family, (not just dutifully but with delight) before pouring his days into the lives of others in his care?

The school was a scant three miles from Maj.'s boyhood home in East Chattanooga. Except for his years at Emory, he stayed close to home, as did son Bud after his own Emory years. For graduate school, Helen ventured as far as the University of Texas at Austin, and in her career as far as Oregon, and then came home.

But when parents dropped off their boys on Missionary Ridge, far from their home, Maj. somehow knew just how hard it was.

Jim Talley was only 12 when he left Knoxville for McCallie in 1936. "Now this is where the impossible task begins. Maj. Burns had an impact at a critical time. Boys growing to manhood needed a father, a pal, a teacher, a counselor, a listener, an idol and a hero. And Maj. was all of these. When my son Jay III came to McCallie in 1960, Maj. meant the same to him. When we were sick, or homesick, Maj. took care of us." But Maj. wasn't only fatherly. Jay Talley continued that "he was warm and tender and handled our crises like a mother would do, but he was firm and strong when situations dictated, like a father."

This called for a constant watchfulness, sometimes rooted in the simple daily act of putting up the mail. Maj. handed boarder Joe Ben Davis a slip of paper as he was leaving French class one day. It read, "See me before you go to football practice."

Davis "was stunned, and a small tremor ran through me. What had I done? My next two classes were a blur. I was about to go home for Christmas my junior year. School and boarding in the dormitory were getting to me. I was not passing anything above a D and did not see much light at the end of the tunnel.

"I went to the O.D. Room and got a 'Close the door, Boy. Sit down, Boy.' And then, 'I have noticed as I have been putting up the mail that you haven't received any mail from home in over six weeks. How are things with your mother?' "

And there it was. "She was getting a divorce and money was about to get tighter."

Maj. continued, "OK. Boy, you will be fine. Check with me every two or three days and tell me how you are doing."

Next Maj. wrote Davis's mother a note. "Joe Ben is a good boy but will have to study hard to graduate." Compassion doesn't cancel out duty.

Ned Giles remembers the warmth of Maj.'s

response when his mother had a stroke, even though Giles was already graduated, and in college. When Jim Speake's grandfather died early in his McCallie career, Maj. advanced him money and got the shaken boy to the plane to get home. Henry Henegar's father died the summer before his junior year. Someone asked whether Maj. had almost seemed like a father after that.

"No," he answered, "Maj. has always been a father to me."

Fathering and mothering don't always involve tenderness or discipline. Parenting often involves turning a boy or girl determinedly toward the road ahead. And that's what happened to Greg Hullender when he lost his father. "Maj. took me aside and talked to me--he had known me since early seventh grade, of course--explaining that I would need to accept more responsibility now, and comforting me with advice." The comfort of advice: hmmmm.

Part of maturing through adolescence is learning to listen to the right voices in addition to your parents. A letter to ALB signed simply Jim, with a return address on the New York Stock Exchange, made this clear.

"It is very difficult for any boy to leave home for the first time. He has to play this off with either a sense of bravado, or abject fear, or perhaps both. Whether he comes from a well supervised home or a non-supervised home, the transition is rather traumatic. Most youngsters have to have something to hold onto and to believe in. You must rely on another human being to build real confidence.

"Some youngsters pick the worst influences with the expected results. Others drift rather aimlessly, usually throughout their lives, and others find a true relationship and have that to build on for the future. Thousands of boys have used you, Maj., as their foundation to build on. I truly wonder what these same thousands would have used as a cornerstone if it hadn't been for Bud Burns.

"I have had the occasion to wonder many times what my life would have turned into without you. Thank God I never had to find out."

McCallie faculty 1926

TITLES
one stuck

Arthur Lee became Bud in the early years of teaching, though Pop stuck for a little while. In 1942 all that changed as World War II began. Many in the class of '42 went off to war instead of off to college, along with them Capt. H. P. Dunlap, who had led the military program that was part of McCallie from 1917 to 1970. Burns, who had been in the ROTC at Emory University and had attended at most an Army Reserve summer camp or two, was promoted to Captain to head the school's military program. He quickly rose to Major, a title commissioned by Dr. Park McCallie (he too, never a military man).

Senator Howard Baker (McCallie '43), said in a speech at McCallie, tongue-in-cheek, that "I was privileged to have served under the tutelage of that great military genius, Major Arthur L. Burns...." Dan Rather, no tongue-in-cheek, called Maj. "a five-star general."

Hanes Lancaster and Jim Talley were visiting

Maj. and Millie at Douglas Hall and as Talley later reminded his mentor, "You showed us your commission papers from Dr. J. P. McCallie. You also modeled your uniform and sucked in your tummy so the blouse would stick out in the proper place. Man, you are a great military figure."

So there.

Major Burns became, shortly, Maj.

"That's as high as I got too, Maj. said. "Dunlap came back from World War II a full colonel. You couldn't have two colonels here."

In 1952 the school named four associate headmasters, none of them McCallies. They were Herbert P. Dunlap, Chalmers M. S. McIlwaine, W. Wallace Purdy, and ALB. A dozen years later he was named dean of students.

"I want it clearly understood," Maj. wrote, "that I was made a dean just as officially as I was made a major several years before. But you know, it never did amount to much. So far as I know, nobody but Col. [DeVere P.] Armstrong, bless his heart, ever referred to me with any consistency as Dean Burns. 'Maj.' was just too firmly entrenched. And that suits me."

For many a legendary figure, one name sticks. Rance Cleaveland wrote in the school newspaper in 1977, "Mention the word McCallie to a McCallie graduate or friend of the school, and, likely as not, he will respond, 'Major Burns.' To many people, Major Burns became the symbol for the school."

Preston Russell confirms this. "Major Burns treated everyone with respectful impartiality, without favoritism, as a duty-bound enforcer of McCallie's tough love and high expectations. Yet his unspoken caring for all of us remains as my most cherished memory over half a century later. I know I am speaking for thousands."

One brand-new alumnus looked 30 years ahead and said, "If I remember anything about McCallie then, it will be Maj." This prophecy fulfilled has created the book in your hands.

In the last days of Maj.'s tenure, an alumnus reported to a friend simply this:

"I've been back to McCallie. I've seen Maj."

This, then, is enough:

Maj.

HONOR
writ small and large

It is worth noting how one encounter, one day, can change everything. And though one day doesn't completely define anybody's character, it can be a sign pointing to the possibility--or the recognition of that quality that calls forth repetition.

Maj. not only insisted on honor, but identified it in action. One day Jack Wiener went to the post office where he received his weekly personal funds, the same prescribed amount deposited by all parents in their boys' accounts. He was stuffing the money in his wallet when he noticed he had an extra dollar. Weiner thought about it and returned the dollar and went to class.

"Later that day," he remembered, "as I was walking to assembly Maj. pulled me aside. 'Jack, you showed me what kind of person you are when you returned that dollar: an honest one.' He told me most boys would not bother returning a dollar. He later told me that I was not only honest but had pride in myself. He was the model of what McCallie tries to make us into."

The lessons in honor prevailed at home as well as at work.

During her high school years, Maj. took Helen to the bus stop in the morning so she could catch the bus for GPS. After she got her driver's license, she wanted to drive those few blocks. One day she decided to cut through the parking lot of Ridgedale Baptist Church, then located at the corner of Union and Dodds Avenues. Her reasoning was that this was a more direct route to the traffic signal at Bailey Avenue. Maj. asked what she was doing, pointing out that this wasn't part of the public street system and that the property belonged to someone else.

After giving her lame reason for the alternate route, she made matters worse by adding: "Besides, it isn't Sunday and the parking lot isn't full. And no one will ever know." In a quiet voice, he said something that has stayed with her always.

"Helen, you know that whether or not you can get away with something has nothing to do with whether it is right or wrong."

John Vickers told on numerous occasions at home and at work what he called "the beautiful story of the time Maj. lost patience with an objectionable little sophomore." Vickers also wrote Maj. to express his thanks for the lesson.

"As the Master of Dormitories you had complete authority and everyone was sympathetic with your objections to this kid. But you felt you had been unjust and you apologized to him in the dining hall in front of the whole student body. In the more than 20 years since that day I have met few men who were big enough or unconceited enough or who had enough sense of humor about life to do the same thing. I thank you for the lesson."

***

Jim Bruce spent three years at McCallie in the 1960s, learning his honorable lessons well.

"I arrived at McCallie in E class (restricted to campus), having not done my summer reading. I don't remember even talking to Maj. until months later when I gained some freedom and was allowed to check out and go to town.

"I got in a rather long line of boys attempting to check out. When I reached Maj. he never looked up from the check-out book and I found I was talking to the top of his head.

" 'Name?' he asked.

" 'Bruce, J. Maj.'

" 'Where you going Bruce?' Long pause.

" 'I don't really know. Maj.' (I remember hearing a number of my fellow students laughing at my answer, apparently knowing what a mistake I had made.)

" 'Where are you going Bruce?'

" 'I thought I'd just go to town and walk around.'

"He had still not looked at me. His eyes were glued to the check-out book. There was silence as I stared at his thinning hair. Suddenly, and with an almost imperceptible initial movement, his head began to move. First to the left and then very slowly back to the right. Gaining speed, back to the left and then to the right. No words, just the movement back and forth--which I decided meant NO.

"The sideways movement stopped. His head began a slow rise to the point that his exasperated eyes met mine. His mouth hung partially open. I'm sure he was asking himself, Why Me Lord?

" 'No.' Pause. 'No.' Pause. 'No, no, no.'

" 'What, Maj.?'

" 'No, no, no, NO!' I stood speechless.

" 'McCallie boys don't go to town to just walk around.'

" 'OK, Maj.'

" 'Where are you going Bruce?' His gaze returned to the book and his pen hand was now hovering mid-air to write my corrected destination.

" 'I think I'll go to the movies.' Maj. knew as well as I did that I still had no idea where I was going.

" 'Do you THINK you are going to the movies or ARE YOU GOING TO THE MOVIES?'

" 'I'm going to the movies Maj.'

" 'Straight and straight, Bruce.'

" 'OK Maj.'

"I was to see that same look numerous times over the next three years. Not always at me, but at someone.

"I finally made Maj. smile before I graduated and it remains a highlight in my life.

"A friend and I had decided to be roommates our senior year. I was then asked to be a prefect. My friend was not asked. I went to Maj. and told him I was turning the job down so I could room with my friend. He looked surprised, disappointed, confused: not sure which. Being selected for prefect was quite the honor and I imagine he got very few turndowns. He asked why and I explained I just wanted to spend my last year with my friend. He asked who my friend was and I told him. Slowly, a smile appeared on his face and he said,

" 'He's a fine boy and you have made a wise decision.'

"Looking back, making Maj. smile and his telling me I had made a wise decision was a milestone I have never forgotten.

"And finally, to my senior year roomie, I wanted you to know that Maj. thought you were a fine boy."

TRUTH
what he expected

"You didn't lie to Maj., and he taught us not to lie to ourselves," said Gene Gwaltney of the man who taught him personal honor. Maj. knew who was telling the truth and who wasn't, and he held that lens up to the honor code.

Mark Rollinson found this out as a seventh grader, when he was reported absent from a class he had in fact attended. New middle schoolers are often given to tears, so when the boy, hurt and confused, went to Major Burns "an insuppressible tear rolled down my cheek as I related my problem and offered to produce witnesses. He casually scratched my name off the list, patted me on the head and in a somewhat stern voice said, 'If you say you were there, you were there.' " That single experience was all young Rollinson needed to know about the honor system: that there is "an immeasurable value to enjoying a reputation for veracity."

Merrill Sexton forgot that he had made a pledge not to leave campus without checking out, and was campused two weeks as a result. A perfect example of learning from your mistakes; "Maj. did me a favor by letting me suffer the consequences of my mistake and reminding me about the importance of keeping your word."

When Robert Pritchett and others were involved in a rock-throwing incident, Maj. took the microphone in chapel. "You know who you are and I know who you are, so it makes sense for you to come tell me."

Enough said, and they did.

Much slips our memories...and then there are the enduring indelibles.

While a student at Sewanee, Revel Lannom went with her father Ted to a spring garden party.

An alumnus mentioned McCallie, but the other guests did not know Ted Lannom's three generations of McCallie connections. Fueled by alcohol, this one man's boisterous talking over-rode the genteel conversations around the patio. The braggadocio concerned his daring escapades in Chattanooga. At a big round table after dinner, the guy bragged about an outing with day students, girls, and cars. When he had returned to campus, he successfully lied to Maj. Burns about where he had been and what he had been up to.

He told of his dishonesty glibly, smoothly. The other guests reacted with "Boys will be boys." "Schools will be schools." "Deans and headmasters will be deans and headmasters."

Ted says, "What got me was the <u>acceptance</u> of the lying as if lying was just a normal part of the McCallie experience."

Ted did not say *I also went to McCallie, and I do not think everybody at McCallie thought lying was OK.*

What Ted did was lock eyes on the guy and say slowly, quietly, deliberately:

"YOU   LIED   TO MAJ. ? !"

It was an awkward moment. The host saw the expression on Ted's face. Revel and Ted stood up and left the table.

Revel was astonished at her father's look. "Dad!"

Ted explained, "Revel, that guy lied to Major Burns and now he is bragging about it!"

This happened in 2012. ALB had been dead 35 years. Indelible influence indeed.

Lee Coward and friends checked out of the dormitory twice in one summer-school week. On the 4th of July, Thursday, they went to Lookout Mountain with a group of girls. The Thursday event involved forbidden alcohol; the second, on Sunday, simply the pleasure of the girls' company. No rule against that. Coward had been at school for only two weeks, and was in lamentable physical condition when he checked in the first night. But somehow Maj. wasn't present at his desk. In his place a student was on duty, so the drinking secret seemed to be safe.

Monday in the cafeteria line Maj. was standing with his usual clipboard, and, when he got to Coward, he said, "Dr. Bob McCallie wants to see you in his office right after lunch." All the boys involved received the same summons.

Dr. Bob's pointed question, "What do you men think about alcoholic beverages in an institution like this?" got Lee Coward into a desperate silent bargaining with God: "Get me out of this and I will never take another drink." But then Dr. Bob said, "It has been brought to our attention that you were drinking alcohol on Sunday."

"We jumped up together and shouted, 'No sir! Not on Sunday!' We denied it because we weren't drinking on Sunday (only on Saturday). And so we went free. Sometimes I wonder whether Maj. adjusted the accusation to Sunday instead of the well-deserved Thursday as a measured act of grace.

"On other occasions we continued enjoying the girls, who picked us up, then brought us back to campus and stayed behind the dormitory and played a little music from their cars.

"Our on-campus adventure stopped the following Monday in chapel when Maj. got up and said, 'Before this gets out of hand I am going to put a stop to it. The girls will have to let you out at my office and leave.'

"He turned from the microphone and looked back in feigned disgust. 'You all are nothing but a bunch of gigolos anyway.'

"I had no idea what a gigolo was.

"I think Maj. knew I was a good boy all along; I just slipped sometimes. At the end of the year my parents came to get me and as I walked out of his narrow office Maj. called me back, put his arm around my shoulder as always and said, 'Lee, you turned out to be a pretty good boy.' I told him I appreciated that and he continued, 'You got off to a bad start last summer.' I again denied the Sunday drinking and his next question was,

" 'How about three days before that?'

"I'll see you next year, Maj."

1976 yearbook cover drawing by Rob Taylor

DUTY

always on

If the life of ALB came to the stage someday, the main set would likely be the narrow perch of the Officer of the Day known as the O.D. Room, where Maj. presided over all goings out and comings in.

First, a boy had to get in line to sign out. Randy Mobley remembers that "He always looked you right in the eye to make sure you understood what was expected of you, and you could just sense his concern for you. The line always backed up, but that was OK, because you knew what was going on at the front of the line: it was Maj. being Maj." Robert Denton will never forget his admonition to go "straight and straight. meaning straight down and straight back from the football game or wherever I was going. He said that to each one of us even though the line might have had 20 or more little boys in it, all eager to go."

Sometimes people came just to watch Maj. in action.

Most boarding students had neither girlfriend nor money, both necessities for going out on a Friday night. Before going to the on-campus movie or to the gymnasium, some boys would line up in the O.D. Room to be entertained by Maj.'s checkout performances. Sometimes recent alumni would show up, pretending to check out. Maj. was not fooled.

One night he was pacing because Ron Harr and Buck Petry were going to Chickamauga lake with a girl whose father owned a very large boat. "I don't like it, I don't like it!" Maj. stormed. "You have done everything you are supposed to do, so I can't do anything about it, and I KNOW you shouldn't go."

Was he right?

"Of course he was," Harr grins.

At evening's end boys had to sign back in. For John Frist, Maj. being Maj. involved a "down-peering gaze, magnified by his glasses as his left middle finger slowly pointed to the clock on the wall which inexplicably had passed the 10 p.m. deadline by minutes."

That same look was a staple of French class as well as check-in. Preston Russell describes it as "rolling his eyes dramatically upward, so that he seemed to look at someone up in the ceiling--or perhaps even heaven--expressing his mock exasperation or disbelief."

Often it was the return that was unforgettable. In Dan Gilchrist's eyes, getting caught coming in late appeared to give Maj. "great delight in peering at me over his glasses. His greatest delight seemed to be inviting me to walk the bullring on the morning before graduation.

"But I did graduate."

Curtis Baggett found himself on the wrong end of a paddle as a new boarder. "We were subject to organized, sanctioned harassment by the older boarders, and new boys were referred to as 'rats.' The responsibilities of rats were two-fold: first, on a rotating basis, one rat per dormitory had to creep into every older boy's room before the rising bells in the morning and turn on the radiator heat without waking the older boys. And second, rats had to pick up the laundry bags of two older boys on Monday mornings and return them, cleaned and pressed laundry inside, on Friday afternoons.

"I was declared errant one week when I didn't get my older boys' laundry back in time because of an extended ninth grade football practice, and I was summoned before the Student Council to atone for my misbehavior. Maj. was the attending faculty member, and I received the customary three licks from a paddle, administered by the first string tackle on the football team. As I was about to get paddled, Maj. turned his head and left the room, as if he couldn't bear to see this inequity. And suddenly, when the pain was at its peak, he reappeared and like a bailiff called for the next case to appear before the kangaroo court. It seemed that Maj. was on my side, but he knew that the system had to be upheld.

"We always felt that Maj. had our best interests at heart, but he had a marvelous gift of chastising us while at the same time putting an arm around us. He had the toughest of all jobs, that of managing hundreds of hormonal teen-age boys and keeping us from self-destruction and getting us to do our best to stay within bounds every day."

This book came to life in an age that forbids corporal punishment, but it reflects a time when sparing the rod was spoiling the boy. Nelson Head's story of a school-sanctioned paddling ends with the writer's assessment of what Maj. was up to.

"Boarding students were hauled up in front of the Student Council for disciplinary violations. Maj. was the adult in the room. We council members were ostensibly in charge--or at least we were led to believe we were. Those boys found guilty were subject to paddling, much like wayward sailors were given lashes. The number of whacks depended upon the severity of the transgression.

"The condemned student was ordered to grab his ankles. One of the members, selected by the president of the council and approved by Maj., was given the broad wooden paddle and administered the punishment to the backside.

"One evening I was selected to administer the punishment. I was new to the process and unsure of my place. The condemned student breathed a sigh of relief when I stood up and took the paddle in hand; there were significantly stronger, older, and more feared members of the council than the gangly sophomore with shaking hands."

WHACK!

" 'Hold on,' Maj.'s irritated and booming voice interrupted. 'That one doesn't count. Head, put more into it.' "

WHACK!

" 'No, no, no! That doesn't count either. What's the matter with you--lean into it and follow through with the paddle.'

"By this time the condemned boy no longer felt relieved."

WHACK AGAIN!--"with much more gusto and follow through.

" 'That's it, now that's one; only four more to go.'

"Maj. was first and foremost a teacher of boys."

Lastly, Maj. also spoke for duty. So it was when Helen took her parents to Jasper, Tenn. to meet

Corry Sharp. She was a land-use planner and he was chair of the Jasper and Marion County Planning Commissions, so they often worked together. The two were also quietly falling in love. Helen explains that "part of why acknow-ledging it took so long was that Corry wanted to protect me from getting into a complex situation. He was raising five children by himself.

"We went to Corry's home, met him and the children; my parents could tell that Corry was smart, warm, kind and fun. On our way back to Chattanooga on old Highway 41, my mother expressed admiration and perhaps amazement that he was raising five children by himself. My father, without in any way minimizing the difficulty of that role, offered this perspective. 'He has done what he had to do. He has done the right thing.' "

Maj. died the following November. Corry and Helen married later that year. He and Millie, whom he called Huggie as her husband had done, were good friends until her death in 1984.

PARADOX
unique alchemy

The French have a proverb, "To understand all is to forgive all." Writer Rod Dreher sees such forgiveness as "a double-edged sword. On the one hand, it tells us that to have perfect understanding is to have perfect forgiveness ...but on the other hand, it tells us that to give oneself over to total sympathy is to lose sight of the reality of evil." ("Dante and the Perils of Pity," The American Conservative, Jan. 14, 2014.)

ALB embodied this proverb. He understood. He forgave. He had total sympathy with the boys. But he also knew behavior has consequences. "You broke the rule. You've got five laps." More colorfully, "If you want to dance, you have to pay the fiddler."

How can inmates enjoy their jailer?

McCallie boys were not really prisoners, but they did not enjoy unfettered freedom. The necessary mechanism to leave campus legally made a lot of them feel incarcerated. Not all students had Maj. for French classes, but all of them had to answer to him for showing up and not showing up at meals, classes, and assemblies. On any school days, there were as many as ten of these appointments.

Often the Please See Me notes were about confirming tardiness or absence. Usually the meeting ended with punishment decreed. But resentment rarely lingered. The McCallie culture was clear: This is what we expect. You did not do it. There is a consequence.

But how could resentment become enjoyment or respect, or even affection?

George Hazard suggests three reasons. "First…he showed boys his respect for them by his very insistence that they get right the dozens of details and responsibilities of McCallie life. He took boys seriously.

"Second, though he wrote the book on those responsibilities, he made the book, by some unique alchemy, go by the heart. Maybe the key was that he spent the energy to make the system's expectations his expectations. Few wanted to fail him.

"Third, he showed that the boys mattered to him by his personal presence in times of personal difficulty as well as of official crisis. Many midnight problems or late check-ins brought [him] to a dormitory at 1 a.m. wearing his overcoat over his pajamas and considerately dismissing the weary teacher on duty.

"But he was on watch at all other times, like the day of return from Christmas vacation when inconsolable young boys would check in at the O.D. Room in North Hall and find him there or in his tiny office under the stairwell. Or maybe he would simply be smoking a Camel cigarette and waiting.

"He would check off the name and offer a handshake or an official-but-sympathetic look with Basset-hound eyes over very smudgy eyeglasses. His face was never a mask. 'Good to have you back, Boy,' he might say calmly before reminding one of the details of supper and bells. 'Supper's at 5:30. It's there for you if you want it.' Perhaps he knew that the routine was the antidote for the trauma of return. Perhaps the boys loved him like the steady father most had left behind. Maybe it was just that Maj. was down there with them, down there in the silent January dusk with them." (*When We Came to The Ridge*, George Hazard Jr., 1991, p. 163)

It was G. K. Chesterton who defined paradox as "truth standing on its head to get attention." It was Major Burns who commanded attention as a living, breathing paradox.

An article in the school newspaper at his death revealed two examples:

"The twinkle in his eye was brightest when he was yelling loudest." And this from a student:

"There were his furies which, somehow, one could fear and not fear at the same time."

As Charlie Battle described it, there was Maj.'s "good-natured wrath."

Chalmers M. S. McIlwaine, also a much-beloved teacher, administrator and associate head-master, arrived with ALB at McCallie in the fall of 1925. In his friend's leading of the Discipline Committee, McIlwaine saw more paradox--or was it more accurately balance?

"Tough and yet gentle, unyielding and yet kind. Phenomenal."

Teaching colleague W. O. E. A. Humphreys recognized two more paradoxes from the faculty side of things: "I can't think of a boy who had anything negative to say about Maj. Oh, they complained about bullring, but never about him. Never any bitterness."

And this: "Sometimes he would have to do some sort of rebuke, and it was always pleasant."

How so? Humphreys saw it as "the unique quality of becoming even more endearing in a burst of his famous anger [because] no cloud of wrath could hide his innate warmth and kindness. For hundreds of old boys these mo-ments must be among their fondest memories of McCallie."

A pleasant rebuke? An adolescent complaint about a punishment *sans* an outcry against the punisher? A complaint without bitterness? A kind anger that became a fond memory?

Yes.

Bestselling author Malcolm Gladwell offers a clue about this paradox in what he calls The Principle of Legitimacy. "Legitimacy is based on three things. First of all, the people who are asked to obey authority have to feel like they have a voice--that if they speak up, they will be heard. Second, the law has to be predictable. There has to a reasonable expectation that the rules tomorrow are going to be roughly the same as the rules today. And third, the authority has to be fair. It can't treat one group differently from another." (*David and Goliath*, Little, Brown & Company, 2013, Kindle Edition, p. 207.)

These three clues lead the reader to one man.

Smile and frown had the same effect, said Joe Stamper. "When he smiled down, put his arm on our shoulder and drew us close to his side, we were securely moored against that impossible problem which led us to him." Likewise "when he frowned, shrugged his arms apart at his sides and created (to us) an imaginary gulf across his office floor because of some infraction, we were guided back to try and cure his hurt and disappointment in us."

For Mills Gallivan, "No matter how bad the message or how bitter the pill to swallow, Maj. always delivered it with compassion and in such a way that you knew he loved you."

Jim Daughdrill Jr. talked about this paradox in a poem, describing his mentor as "always with a coat and tie, but never dressed up; always a teacher, but never a scholar; always a humble man, but never was one made who could get as mad and yell as loud; always a teacher of values, never just a teacher of French."

Here's an embodied truth: Justice and mercy can achieve the same goal.

So it was at McCallie with the practice of paddling for minor infractions, a method thoroughly out of use in the 21st century. For a junior schooler who broke a rule, the punishment would be licks with a paddle, and those licks were administered by older boys, and not without pain. Major Burns as head of the Discipline Committee was present for those sessions, and this is how one older boy described it. "Maj. would put the boy's head on his shoulder and pat him on his back as the paddling was administered. He knew the boy was going to cry, because the punishment would be carried out."

Justice and mercy sometimes came at the same time, from the same man.

Here's a final paradox: he was a world-wise hometown boy. Only the physical geography of his life hinted at provincialism. Curious mind and understanding heart reached broad and deep, marking ALB a man of the world.

MUSIC
a little on the loud side

McCallie's Alma Mater

McCallie, dear McCallie School
Thy loyal sons are we;
Strong in thy strength we'll ever stand,
And true we'll always be.
In thee we place our fondest trust,
For thee our prayers shall rise;
Oh, Alma Mater, hail, all hail!
We lift our song to thee;
Oh, Alma Mater, hail, all hail!
We lift our song to thee.
—Arthur L. Burns '20

It was 1930 when Arthur L. Burns penned his school's Alma Mater (Latin for nourishing or nurturing mother). Was Maj., who taught Latin in his first McCallie year, chosen for this task because he understood what it meant to be an *alma mater?*

The school website offers a scratchily authentic recording of Maj. teaching the song to the students, along with some guidelines for a respectful presentation.

He began, "Dr. Bob McCallie asked me--well, I don't think I asked to be allowed to do this, though I'm capable of it--to present the Alma Mater and teach it to the boys. We don't have to approach it on our knees or anything like that, but let's don't take too many liberties with it so as to be tempted to get out of line when an important event comes along.

"By the way, the music is all right. I had nothing to do with it. It's all right." (He borrowed the tune from "The Prince of Pilsen.")

And so he led, admonishing the boys to sing the final "Hail, All Hail" and all other farewell hymns "not as dirges, but with a little more balance."

Sometimes he suggested singing "a little on the loud side." A little? As Rance Cleaveland remembers, he encouraged the boys "in a sly and funny way to sing LOUD, THE LOUDER THE BETTER! That blood-thumping shout of 'HAIL, ALL HAIL' was so energizing, and so much fun." The key word in this process was balance: respect with exuberance.

John G. Varner, a fellow faculty member and later a professor at the University of Texas at Austin, saw here a clue to ALB's understanding of boys. Sing, even shout, in unison, but always temper it with respect.

Randy Mobley claims he can still sing the Alma Mater like the day he graduated, "because of Maj.'s impact on all of us when he stepped forward to teach it to the new students each year. It was the single most anticipated event in the McCallie student assembly each fall. When we hit the second 'Hail, All Hail' you could almost feel the chapel roof rattle."

Maj. wasn't just partial to his own tune. Although he may have liked classical music and opera in high school, at Emory it became a passion. In the early 1920s Burns' contemporary L.H. Gross made his first solo road trip. He went from his home in Fort Payne, Ala. to Atlanta where he spent the night at the Kimball House at Five Points.

"There I was, an ignorant country boy eager to see the sights of a big city and to hear GRAND OPERA. I remember [ALB] came by the hotel and visited with me. We kept up a good-natured raillery over who was the better singer, Martinelli or Gigli."

In his McCallie French class Burns played a record of "The Marseillaise" and led the boys in singing—en Francais. He was often charged by the headmasters with instilling culture in what Tom McCallie described as a most uncultured student body, and he began those afternoon assemblies with the very word.

"Dr. McCallie has asked that I teach you boys some culture."

It might be an all-school assembly lightly billed as "Burns Brushes off Beethoven." For George McCall, "Aida" in the company of Maj. was "the only opera I ever enjoyed."

Jim Speake, who ended up in the theater business in New York, always loved music, but it was Maj. who gave him a love of opera. Others might not have caught the opera love, but not for want of a teacher. Here's how ALB introduced a favorite, "La Boheme."

"You will hear these words, 'Mimi, why are your little hands so cold?' That is because Mimi was dying of consumption."

Spencer McCallie III was there, and smiling at the man's cleverness. "In this way he was teaching us that she doesn't SOUND like she's dying because it's opera. It was funny--everything about it was funny--and a beautiful introduction to opera, where nothing is as it seems."

David McLain discovered that Maj.'s favorite hymn was "A Mighty Fortress is our God," and learned moreover from Maj.'s life the meaning of the whole stanza. To ALB, God <u>was</u> "a bulwark never failing." By Maj.'s own request, that hymn was played at his funeral along with "O God Our Help in Ages Past" and "Sing with All the Sons of Glory"—with the familiar dictum that they would be sung "a little on the loud side."

Music was a common theme in correspondence. During World War II John Vickers recounted his time as a soldier and his love for Italy. He knew Maj. would want to know "about the music in Rome. I speak truly when I say that by comparison the Metropolitan sounds like a road company. We went to 'Faust.' Really, it was the nearest thing to perfection that I have ever heard. I don't expect to hear its equal again until the next life unless, of course, I manage to get back to Rome again."

Maj. kept that letter, and knew whereof Vickers spoke.

If ALB had organized his music with iTunes, Helen says a favorite playlist would include:

"McCallie Alma Mater"
  sung by students, composed by ALB

"Now Thank We All Our God"
  Quincy Choral Society

"Joyful, Joyful We Adore Thee"
  Mormon Tabernacle Choir

"Love Lifted Me"
  Londonderry Choir

"A Mighty Fortress is Our God"
  Joslin Grove Choral Society

"O God, Our Help in Ages Past"
  Westminster Abbey Choir

"Sing With All the Saints in Glory"
  WLP Choir

"Se Quel Guerrier lo Fossi!"
  Aida, Act I, Luciano Pavarotti

"Si, Mi Chiamano Mimi"
  La Boheme, Act I Scene VI, Grace Moor

"La Marseillaise"
  Jacques Gautier

"Hard Times Come Again No More"
  James Taylor and Yo-Yo Ma

"Wreck of the Old 97"
  Norman Blake

"Take Me Out to the Ballgame"
  Harry Caray

GRACE
if not straight and straight

Herman Hunter was one of countless boys who received grace, pure unmerited favor. He was brought before the faculty for disciplinary reasons, and several faculty members wanted to expel him. Major Burns stood up for Hunter and insisted on a second chance. "This amazed me," Hunter wrote to Maj., "because you were the one who had caught me and gave me a lecturing I shall never forget! I wanted you to know that one of your troublemakers from the 1950s thinks you were the guiding light."

There were times when a boy wasn't making trouble, but having troubles that were hard to talk about. In his first year as a boarder, Robert Moore had a visit from his mother telling him that she and his father were divorcing. "I was very upset and confused about how this was up-ending my family. Back in that day in the South, divorces were unheard of among folks that I knew.

"I remember standing outside of Maj.'s office, looking at the student roster which listed our parents and our home addresses. I needed to see if there was any evidence of other McCallie boys who came from divorced families. There was no indication that anyone else shared my fate. As an impressionable 14-year-old, new to the school, I didn't know what to do. Maj. was the only person I felt comfortable to talk with about my embarrassment and humiliation. He understood my feelings and agreed not to reflect my parents' changed situation on the roster. As I recall, this was not done until 1956, by which time I had adjusted to a new family reality."

There was one area of, shall we say, vulnerability, that evoked a regular grace-giving. It happened on Sunday when the Burns family finally sat down to a long-awaited afternoon lunch at home, the only family time they could ever depend on in the long week of a dean of students. Invariably the phone would ring and it would be a boarding student who no doubt had just met some girl at church, and would offer this pitiful tale of how he had forgotten to check out for a Sunday afternoon off campus. Would Maj. please check him out in absentia? Maj. would fuss loudly at the boy and grouse about why the boy hadn't done it earlier, more timely, and more in accordance with the rules. After reading the riot act to the boy for pulling this stunt every Sunday for the last six weeks, he would return to the dinner table, to Millie and Bud and Helen, laughing.

Curtis Baggett explains that "every boy knew that Maj. was a pushover when it came to courting a pretty girl on a sunny fall afternoon off campus. (After all, that was how he had met Millie.) So he was accustomed to giving the appropriate complaining voice, then smiling to himself, all the time wishing the boy good luck with his new-found girlfriend."

In the ordered world of a boarding school, seconds count. For David Phillips, the just count was occasionally overruled by grace. "I was one of the boarding students who had a steady local girlfriend who attended GPS. Naturally, I checked out on a date every chance I got. I was almost always running late to curfew and hit the door running. He would be looking at his watch as I stood panting before him listening to a host of sarcastic remarks such as, 'two seconds early tonight'. More than once, I know he misread his watch a little to keep from punishing me. We always knew he wanted us to think he was a lot tougher than he really was. He loved us and we loved him!"

David Thompson writes: "I'll never forget 1960 when McCallie won the football game over the state champions and a vacation was declared for Monday. Maj. helped me get home by advancing my airplane fare. A few years later, I neglected to submit my blue slip on leaving for Christmas vacation. The telephone was ringing as I got home. Maj. called to see if I had arrived. His fairness and sense of judgment and justice will be long remembered."

7 Dec '44

Dear Mr. Burns,

Just a few lines to let you know that I'm still around. Right now I'm in a Paris Hosp. I hurt my left knee a little a few days ago while up in Germany knocking on Hitler's back door. However it's not bad, and I'll be back in a few days.

I'm sorry I haven't had time to write before. If you get a chance, Please drop me a line and let me know how ~~the~~ everyone is. I hope it won't be too long before I can pay you a visit.

Harry landed on Leyte. He and MacArthur - "have Returned".

My Regards to Mrs A.L. and "Little Bud."

Pete Branton

WAR
co-respondent

In a box in the Burns archives rests a treasure trove of stationery, crumbling at the edges with the weight of years since World War II, specifically the years between 1942 and 1950. The letters came from return addresses in Italy, the Philippines, the Southwest Pacific; they were written on ship, at the Navy Medical Center, at Camp Lejeune. Millie saved the letters to ALB, especially the ones beginning with the graduates of 1942, because most of them went into the Army, Navy, or Marines instead of going to college. Their training and deployments spanned the globe.

The letters had common threads:
- apology for not writing sooner
- thanks for ALB's letter
- greetings to Millie, Bud Jr., and later to little Mary Helen
- greetings to Mr. Pressly, Mr. Tate, Mr. Spence McCallie, Mr. Bob McCallie, Mr. McIlwaine, and Mr. Purdy

It appeared that naming the other teachers meant ALB was the only former teacher they were corresponding with. Obviously other teachers received letters, but one could describe his wartime function as a one-man alumni office. Maj. was for his boys, as one said, "the glue that held us together in the war years." In this way he became a war correspondent.

One five-page missive arrived on stationery from Adams House at Harvard in 1945. John Vickers, back from the war, expressed a respectful dubiousness about the popular value of an excellent education—and offered a higher purpose that fits both McCallie and Harvard. He wrote to Maj.

"In spite of the fact that I appreciate it more [than before the war] I don't think that this kind of education is nearly as important as I once thought that it was. In fact, I doubt that any of it is much good except for the chance that it gives you to come into contact with fine men. If a school or university hasn't got any men of character, as far as I'm concerned they just may as well close shop no matter how many experts they may have in this or that field. I doubt I shall learn anything in my courses here or in the seminary that will help me to be a better minister. The thing I shall get is the contact with the few men who are really great that I would not have otherwise gotten to meet."

One more proof that example--both male and female--is the best teacher.

Bud's war correspondents whose letters survive include this roll call: Lloyd Baxter, Roderick Beddow, Irwin Belk, Bill Benoit, Frank Bird, Elliott Blaydes, Pete Branton, Mac Bridger, Henry Carrington, Joe Coffield, Jimmie Corn, Bob Dobyns, Bill Dunn, Dee Dunn, Jakie Dunn, Murdock Dunn, Tom Eichelberger, Breck Ellison, John Ed Faucette, Julian Ficklen, Lanham Frazier, Cecil Garrett, Phil Gibbs, James Gillespie, Joe Harper, Bob Harris, Theo Harvey, Thomas Hendrick, Dean Hudson, Terrell Huggins, Warren James Jr., Warren James Sr., Charles Jarrett, Dick Johnson, Carl Kincaid, Dick Koella, Bob Lambert, Hanes Lancaster, Winston Linam, Dooley Lothrop, Dick McCubbin, Doug Millar, Jim Millis, Benji Morris, Buck Moseley, Houston Patterson, Gene Peek, Phinizy Percy, Osborne Perry, J. B. Ramsey, Craig Robinson, Gene Schimpf, Nick Senter, Jack Shannon, Alf Sharp, Sonny Sherrill, Harold Sibold, Bob Sims, Robert Smitherman, Walt Stamper, Gerry Stephens, John Ed Stone, Paul Swank, Hugo Taliaferro, Jim Talley, Mark Thompson, Charles Vernon, John Vickers, David Walke, Bobby Walker, Calvin Wells, Pat Williams, and Trent Zeppa.

Sixty-four McCallie men died in this war, from Commander Thomas Calloway Latimore '11, nine years Maj.'s senior, to Maj.'s student PFC Ben Bob Ross of the class of 1944. The class of 1942 lost ten members. Among those who gave their lives were Tommy Hendrick, Richard Henry Johnson, Robert Smitherman and Paul Swank, whose letters to Maj. survive. Letters from Carrington, Dee Dunn, Frazier, Johnson, Lancaster, Millar, Percy, Sims, and Talley were many over many years.

Boarders Branton and Lancaster married Chattanooga girls. About one-third of these writers sent sons to study under ALB at McCallie. Second and third generation surnames continue to mark the rolls and the awards given at school, including two awards that honor names on the war roll.

The Thomas Winchester Hendrick Christian Leadership Award was given for years in memory of Hendrick.

Gibbs paid for the J. Philip Gibbs French Medal, but he gave it as a tribute to ALB.

McCubbin, one of many McCallie-grown educators, was headmaster of The Casady School in Oklahoma City in the 1980s.

WORLD WAR II

PVT CHARLES SUMPTER WYLIE '43
PFC MORRIS BELKNAP MOORMAN '43
PFC JOHN TURNER GRAVES '43
PFC JAMES PERRY HARTNESS, JR '43
PFC EDWARD GILBERT TALIAFERRO '43
CPL CHARLES HARWOOD MOORMAN '43
2LT GEORGE THOMAS BRIGHT '43
PFC BEN BOB ROSS '44

19

SMOKE
he did and knew if you did

Maj. himself smoked cigarettes; in those days there was no general caution for adult use of tobacco. There was among faculty, however, a hearty respect and not a little fear of co-founder Dr. Park McCallie, who did not approve. Often the telltale glow of a cigarette caught Dr. Park's watchful eye.

Latin teacher W. O. E. A. Humphreys spoke thus of the Doctor: "His Christian faith, revealed in his daily life, not just in his words, was a powerful force. Doctor wielded authority with assurance born of deep and unshakeable conviction." For these reasons teachers were careful not to smoke in Doctor's presence.

A school has a heart as well as a soul, and Humphreys continued that "If the soul of McCallie reposed in Doctor's keeping, the heart of the school was in the gruff but gentle care of Major Burns." Heart would never disrespect soul.

One Friday supper in the dining hall--Maj. was always early--so the legend goes, Maj. lit up. He had plenty of time to finish his Camel before teachers and students were supposed to arrive. But then Dr. Park appeared! He was never expected in the cafeteria on a Friday night. Hastily Maj. abandoned the cigarette near the stainless tubing of the cafeteria line. But not hastily enough.

"Arthur Lee!" boomed Dr. Park. "Whose cigarette is that?"

The account that follows may be a futile attempt to put a chink in ALB's burnished armor.

The story goes--though one cannot be sure--that Maj. examined the cigarette and burst out, "Why Doctor, that must be John Day's cigarette!"

Could a holy fear have sabotaged this most honorable of men? All we know is that such a thing is possible. Col H. P. Dunlap told a story of a distinguished speaker on campus, the chaplain of the U.S. Senate. After his address the two went up on the side of the ridge behind Dr. Park's house, where it was late enough, dark enough and safe enough to smoke.

Ron Harr and Buck Petry were not the only boys who conjured up what they believed to be a foolproof plan. As school photographers they did their smoking in the darkroom in the basement of Founder's Home. If anyone, teach-er or student, knocked, they bought time to cover their tracks by calling out, "We can't open the door. We are developing pictures!"

The plan worked well enough, until one day Harr emerged from the darkroom to find Maj. nearby. "Maj. put his arm around me, as he often did. Sort of a headlock. And then he drew me close to his side, which was the last thing I wanted right then.

" 'Ronnie Boy,' he chided. 'You are far too fine a boy to be smoking cigarettes' "

Mitch Taylor got caught slightly more red-handed, or red-pocketed. "I was 15 years old and living in Maclellan Hall for summer school. A couple of buddies and I were smoking in a second floor dormitory room when I glanced out the door and saw Major Burns drifting silently down the hall. However, he kept going and did not return to the room of then-panicked kids.

"I rammed the burning cigarette into my short pants and turned the fan on supersonic to rid the room of any evidence of the odious deed. We all began to relax, thinking we had pulled the wool over the old guy, when out of nowhere he appeared like a shadow and warned me, 'Boy, you had better get the cigarette out of your pocket before you burn yourself.'

"How he knew or how he reappeared remains a mystery. But I was put in E class yet again and my parents notified that I was on the slippery slope to hell."

John David Hopkins was a freshman in Douglas Hall, where he thought a wet mattress from a spilled Coke could be dried out with the heat from his secret lights-out reading lamp. He awoke with his mattress on fire. He dragged it to the shower across the hall, put out the fire and went back to sleep. He had a hard time convincing Maj. the next day that the fire did not start with a lit cigarette.

Not everybody got caught. Pete McCall was the erstwhile chaplain of the McCallie Smoking Club, which meant "my job was to pray Major Burns wouldn't catch us puffing on cigarettes in our parents' cars in the chapel parking lot."

For day student Gary Beene, his usual worry was whether he was wearing the regulation belt of his uniform. That changed on the day he fainted in Maj.'s presence. In those days boarders could smoke with parental permission. Beene was in the dormitory, without permission to be present OR to smoke. Curiosity got the best of him, and he took a long drag. At that moment Maj. walked in. The boy held in the smoke as long as possible. And then, he says, "I fell over like a dead man. I had fainted, and at this point the remaining smoke leaked out of my nose and mouth. I faintly [he meant that literally] recall that Ronnie Thomas said to Maj. that he had scared me to death."

Beene revived, and the next step was vintage ALB. "Maj. gave me room to repent and own up to my error and after a long night at home I came back the next morning and made my way into Maj.'s office to confess all. I will never forget his larger-than-life appearance to me. The one thing I did not want to do was disappoint this man. There was something so very different about him that would not allow me to compromise. I took his discipline which was tempered by my confession."

Some days never lose their luster in a man's story. More than half a century later, Beene reflected that "we were all beneficiaries of a special soul and spirit in Major Burns, and that just gets better for me as the days go by."

Timing was everything. Sometimes Maj. just waited. Frank Kollmansperger cited an unforgettable day, "the day after graduation, when he reiterated for me all the things that our gang had done for the whole year, all of which we thought we had gotten by with. Isn't it an amazing thing that he had left these things undone and unsaid until the end?"

No one who knew Maj. would believe his timing was accidental. He had his reasons for immediacy; he had reasons just as surely for a delay.

Three boarders thought they were returning the big McCallie bus to its place beside the infirmary before anyone would note its absence. They had had a midnight joy ride on Lookout Mountain, perhaps with girlfriends. As they got off the bus, Maj. came by on his normal early-morning walk to his office. "Morning, boys," is the only greeting they got. What happened later is another story, not for inclusion here.

***

Joe Ben Davis and two buddies skipped campus one Sunday evening to get Krystal hamburgers on Brainerd Road. As they walked back through the Missionary Ridge tunnel, Maj. drove by and looked right at them. Monday morning came. Then Monday afternoon assembly. No Please See Me note. Tuesday--nothing. By Wednesday afternoon Joe Ben had been near-sleepless for three nights. Finally Maj. called them in.

"You did not think I was going to let you get by with it, did you?'

For Joe Ben and most others whose apprehension for a misdemeanor has been protracted, the delay increases the punishment. There is another kind of apprehension at work. Yes, Maj. knew that.

ALB's parents, John Anderson Burns and Minnie Huffaker Burns, married in 1901. Their North Chamberlain Avenue home in East Chattanooga. LEFT: Brother Eddie B Burns and Arthur Lee Burns about 1907.

On this corner in Chattanooga, at the George K. Brown Palace at Market and 7th Streets, ALB first saw 18 year-old Mildred Cooley. The following July of 1928, she eloped with the 26 year-old teacher and did not return to Girls Preparatory School for her senior year.

The Daytona vacation sponsored by Millie's mother, Mrs. Cooley. Millie, Helen, and Bud Jr. with ALB. ALB was ready to return home passing Ringgold.   BELOW: Bud Jr. as a seventh grader with his father, 1949.

FACING PAGE: ALB in his North Hall office next to the O.D. Room, 1957. ALB counting laps at the Alumni Field bullring. Even when distracted, he knew who cut the curves. "You lost that lap, boy."

A surprised ALB and Millie are presented a trip to France as a gift initiated by the Class of 1961. Below, the note Helen has kept since college.

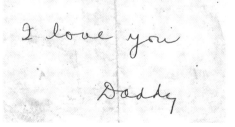

ALB in his Caldwell Hall office and with Markham Smith and Jack Grimes. ALB presented Helen at the Girls Cotillion in 1967. See the edge of this picture on Maj.'s desk.

PREVIOUS: The top picture behind ALB shows Douglas Hall and Middle Hall in ALB's student days. LEFT: Directing 1972 graduation with Steve Killian. ABOVE: At least it was only a single telephone. BELOW: Receiving a special Keo-Kio award at retirement.

Middle Hall was the sole classroom building when ALB enrolled in 1916. It came down in 1974 in favor of the quadrangle in front of the new academic building, which by 1976 contained the Burns Student Center. In 2010, a state-of-the-art dormitory high on the Ridge and south of everything was dedicated in memory of ALB.

BURNS HALL

TOP: On the Alumni Hall steps: Hal Daughdrill as a senior in 1973, ALB, and Jim Daughdrill '52, then president of Rhodes College. LEFT: ALB in 1970 with grandson Lee. BELOW: 2013 in Memphis: Hal Daughdrill, former chairman of McCallie trustees, Lee Burns '87, and Jim Daughdrill with Russell portrait of ALB.

TOP: Helen Burns Sharp and Corry Sharp at the Bluff View Art District in Chattanooga. UPPER RIGHT: Bud Burns Jr. '55, Helen Burns Sharp, and their Aunt Katherine Burns. Katherine married for the first time at age 52. She said she liked marriage so well that she wished she had married at 50. BOTTOM: ALB and Keo-Kio members at the 1972 retirement ceremony honoring ALB.

Seven Burns children, their mother, mates and progeny, 2013: Encircling the bride and groom, May and Jeff Burke: Jim and Andrea Burns: Ellie, Syd and Edy Gervin; Dillon and Lucy Rose. Graham Walker Burns (mother of the bride). Bennett Kutchins, Carol Burns Stoney. Graham Smith Burns, Lee and Sarah Burns. Children on the front row: Catherine and Caroline Burns, Graham Gervin, Walker and Ward Rose. Arthur and Preston Burns. Alexandra Kutchins and Betsy Burns.

BULLRING

why not just walk to Atlanta?

John McCall found this entry in the 1950 school yearbook: "Maj. reminds Charlie Gaar that he can't leave until he has walked off his 286 laps on the bullring. Gaar asks if he can't just walk to Atlanta instead."

Lew Conner's "well-deserved punishment" sent him back to McCallie many Saturday mornings to walk the bullring with Maj., where he was being taught that "failure to follow the rules has consequences, that life would be better if I chose the correct path." In the process Maj. became his friend and counselor, for bullring was one more method the watchful dean used to find out who needed him. As he outgrew bullring, having learned its lessons, Conner "often sat in Maj.'s small office, talking with him about life there academically, athletically and in general. He seemed to have an endless ability to listen to my problems and those of so many others. He then gave superb counsel. Maj.

always had time for all of us."

Franklin McCallie was a student of Maj.'s who made a careful study of the administrator in preparation for becoming principal of Kirkwood High; here he explains and justifies the bullring.

"At McCallie during Major Burns' tenure, there was a hallowed institution called the bullring, established with the understanding that some students just cannot manage all the rules. Students who had received certain marks or demerits for the preceding week had the unique privilege of taking their Saturday afternoons by walking in laborious circles around the school track. The number of laps to be walked on a 440-yard track depended on the level of infraction that a student had committed against school rules. Running was not acceptable as that might have enabled a student to miss certain instructive minutes considering why he might not want to make the same mistake that brought him to the bullring on this day.

"While the bullring might have been good for a student's physical health, certain students had other plans for their Saturday afternoon, reason enough to attempt to speed up or cut down the number of laps. This, however, was difficult, since Major Burns sat up in the concrete bleachers and kept fastidious notes.

"So what was an enterprising McCallie boy to do? I never walked the bullring, but I often had reason to see it at work. There were only two sure-fire methods of cutting down on the time or the distance necessary to walk. Both methods depended on waiting until a student got between Maj. and some parts of the bullring, or when Maj. was looking down at his official records.

"In the first method, a sly student would attempt to get 10 to 20 quick strides on the track to speed up the bullring process. This student had to quit the run in time, or Maj. saw the last few strides.

"The other method was more creative, since it cut down the total distance needed to complete the day. At one end of the track the pole vault lane cut across the curve at the end of the oval, and if a bullring participant could see that Maj. was preoccupied with a large number of students, he could hoof it down that path and get to the other side before Maj. saw him.

"There was a recurring problem, however. Maj. was sometimes not so intently watching the student nor astutely marking down the accomplished laps as he was bending his eyes--not his face--toward the McCallie Avenue side of the track, just enough to see feet moving a little too fast or a straight line being cut across the oval.

"There was no shout, no sign of recognition. However, when the offending student came around and was in place for Maj. to give him credit for the lap, Maj. would say in a calm voice--even fatherly:

"You lost that lap, Boy."

Bullring was a reality for late arrivals and for high-achievers alike on the morning before graduation. It was graduation day of 1969 and Robert Kirk Walker Jr., who 30 years later would become the first non-McCallie family headmaster, had the valedictorian's address to deliver at the Sunday ceremony.

But first, thanks to Major Burns, Walker had to walk the bullring.

This is how he tells it:

"Two days before graduation, I borrowed the school's Chevy Impala to go to the Times Printing Company to finish getting the final issue of the Tornado ready for print. As usual, it took longer that I had hoped. I returned to campus after 11:00 that evening and called my parents to take me home.

"The next morning, upon my arrival at school, I was summoned to Maj.'s office. He informed me that I had neglected to return the car key to its designated spot. I apologized, handed him the key, and explained the lateness of the hour. He said: 'It's still five demerits.' He then looked at me and said: 'I suppose you're thinking about using your quality points to remove those demerits.' I replied that since I had never used any of them before, it seemed like an appropriate time to do so. He then said: 'Unfortunate timing. I cleared all of them last night.' When I asked what that meant, he replied that I would need to walk the bullring.

"Early on the morning of Commencement, I was walking around the track, and Maj. was supervising my efforts. After about four laps, he said: 'Time served.' We both grinned and went on with the rest of our day. Lesson learned: A rule is a rule, and exceptions should only be made when there is a compelling reason to do so. Thank you, Maj, for providing me with an almost pleasant way to learn it."

At the ALB funeral in 1977, parking was a problem around First-Centenary United Methodist Church. From near Atlanta, Joe Ben Davis had driven about 150 miles and entered the sanctuary a few minutes late. His first thought was, "I guess I'll have to walk some laps on the bullring to make up for this."

PERFORMER

always on

Perhaps it all began in 1937, when a student dramatic production of Booth Tarkington's musical "Seventeen" included two faculty members—William Pressly and Arthur Burns. It continued with Burns in many venues, most notably the O.D. Room, assembly and chapel.

"Dadgumit! Dadgumit!" usually signaled accumulated frustration with boys' misbehavior.

Hearing the repeated word, witnesses would report in the dormitories, "Maj. is on a crud."

If you planned to check out, you would prepare accordingly. If you were staying on campus, you might go to the O.D. Room to watch the show.

Tom Drew was one of many who went down to the O.D. Room to enjoy the evening show. "Maj. was always on. He loved to entertain, was extremely compassionate and treated the 'good' boys and the 'bad' boys all alike. Sometimes boys had special permission to leave, and when you brought the signed blue document, he would give you that pained expression, or if it had been a particularly difficult day he might throw a pencil. He would probably mimic your tone: 'Maj., I want to check out.' You would smile and enjoy the show."

He treated the good and bad boys alike because they were on the same list for him.

Curtis Baggett remembers Maj. onstage at assembly.

"Every fall when new boys arrived, Maj. taught us how to stay on the legal side of required church attendance. We got to choose our church, which usually amounted to which church had the most girls. There were always a few boys who wanted to attend First-Centenary United Methodist Church, which presented a problem. Most boys and most families who picked up boarders in the Sunday morning ride line on McCallie Avenue attended First Presbyterian Church, which meant that their ride stopped a block from First-Centenary. Maj.'s elaborate demonstration was performed on the stage, and boys who were nervous and already lost in a city they knew nothing about were mesmerized. To Maj., the way to demonstrate a walk to First-Centenary was to leave First Presbyterian, walk west down McCallie Avenue to the very end, turn around and walk back east a block to First-Centenary on their left. Never mind that they had already passed First-Centenary on their right!"

Maj.'s showmanship invited a response from the boys. Sandy McMillan offers an example.

"Maj. stood at the lectern. His announcement went something like this, 'Now, boys, I know that McCallie boarders who have their parents' permission may smoke in designated areas. However, lately we have discovered that some boys are chewing tobacco and dipping snuff. Boys, McCallie will not be known as a tobacco chewing or snuff dipping school!' To emphasize his last statement, he spoke very slowly and emphasized each syllable. As he emphasized each syllable, he shook his hand toward the student body. By the time he repeated this statement with the accompanying gestures, the entire student body was gesturing in unison with him."

During one summer school session, Spencer McCallie III announced a series of Wednesday evening foreign films. Rob Betz, George Marshall and other boarders, considering this a potentially exciting development, wanted to know more and knew who could tell them. They prepared their questions and showed up in Maj.'s office, but somehow in his presence they were speechless. Betz begins, "George and I found Maj. that late afternoon in his office. Though he was usually behind his desk working on his lists, we found him instead resting in his orange leatherette chair--his head thrown back, evidently 'resting his eyes' as he sometimes did.

" 'What do you boys need?' he asked after open-ing one eye to ascertain which of his many charges had presented themselves at his door. Maj. could raise his voice if he was mad. He had a wide range of ways that he communicated. Sometimes I thought he was just a great listener--which he was. Other times, I thought he was just making the best of a theatrical moment--skillfully used to impress something particular upon you.

"Maj. worked with boys. He knew boys. Most McCallie boys that knew him were convinced that Major Burns was up late each night working on his particular problems. Sensing the difficulty of our question, without opening his eyes Maj. said 'Why don't you sit down and maybe it will come to you?'

"Shoeless George and I sat on the orange couch next to his chair, leaned forward and I said, 'Maj, we understand that there are going to be foreign films shown above the cafeteria. George, me, and some of the guys were wondering if you could tell us a little more about it?'

"He again opened one eye to look at George and me. While never moving his head from his resting place on the back of his chair, he shut both eyes, crossed his chest with his arms above his short-sleeve white business shirt, over the dark tie--and said, 'Young Spencer has a dream. A dream of a boy--a cultured boy--whose horizons will be expanded reading subtitles. Subtitles from words spoken by some foreign actor, no doubt chewing the scenery of some literary classic.'

"The room went silent again. His eyes were shut, and his head was still leaning back. We could not tell if Maj. was smiling, even just a little. George asked, 'Maj, is that it?'

"Maj, again with closed eyes, inscrutably said, 'That's it.' "

Maj. practiced a good bit of showmanship during summer school assemblies, a talent that hearkened back to hours at home watching "The Jack Benny Show." Witnesses asked the family, "Is he that funny at home?" Their answer: Yes. Maj. was humorous in conversations at home, but being literally onstage called for a different kind of wit. Example: Maj. was also caretaker of almost everything else that needed to be announced. He <u>was</u> the Lost and Found. One day he held up a lost set of swim goggles, asking the owner to come get them "because they are scaring me."

NUMBERS

man of letters, man of numbers

Maj. taught French and his colleague C. M. S. McIlwaine taught mathematics. They had joined the faculty together in 1925 and were promoted to associate headmasters together in 1952. Maj.'s nickname for CMSM was "Preacher," but they both taught adult Sunday school classes downtown. Maj. taught at First-Centenary United Methodist, and CMSM taught at Central Presbyterian. CMSM was a mathematics wizard, able to perform complex computations in his head. But one day in French class, Maj. claimed he was not all that bad with numbers himself. He proceeded to fill a six- or eight-foot chalkboard with about a dozen rows of 12-digit numbers. Then, only glancing at each column right-to-left, he added the colossal sum in just a few seconds. Then he turned to the class: "Check me."

"We did," says one of those boys, "and his sum was accurate."

Perhaps ALB almost understood only logarithms, but he had calculated the sum of many things.

In 1930 associate headmaster Dr. Thomas Edward Peck Woods invented the Privilege Rating System. Every other Wednesday, students were rated in A Class, B Class, C Class, D Class, or E Class (0-49 percent). Scholarship average minus penalties plus bonus (for no penalties) equaled a boy's rating. A grade of A was assigned 95 points, B--85 points, and so on down to E, which was assigned 50. The rule book stated, "Unless a boy received penalties he cannot earn E Class, since the lowest scholarship grade is 50." Computations were made by the school recorder, the daughter of Dr. Woods, Miss Zella Woods. She wrote the rule book.

Her computations drove much of ALB's workload, especially on Saturdays, when all D Class and E Class boys were required to report to Study Hall at 9:00 a.m. E Class boys were required to come back to Study Hall from 12:50 to 2:50 p.m.

Like logarithms, ALB ironically said he "almost understood the Privilege Rating System."

Aside from mathematics, the rule book had one simple negative rule: "No boy, day or boarding student, may leave the campus during school hours without checking out with Major Burns." The name of Major Burns was stated six more times in the rules about attendance. You didn't report to an office, but to a man, one man. He was ever present.

Longtime baseball fans had radio, one game a week on television, and newspapers to keep up. Maj.'s favorite team, the St. Louis Cardinals, had Stan Musial. Maj. would check the box score in the newspaper during the week and compute Musial's batting average just for his own edification.

Tiger Jones says he too was a big St. Louis Cardinal fan "and we used to talk about the Cardinals a lot. When I graduated I thought so much of Maj. that I gave him my baseball autographed by Stan Musial."

In the 1940 census, ALB listed his hours worked per week at 99. Daughter Helen feels sure he fudged. Though he was a supremely honorable man, his daughter wondered aloud, "Does anybody think Maj. ever worked that few hours?"

ALB's prime photographer, Ron Harr,
visited from college.

MINIMAL
see?

This chapter will have to be short, by definition. But here's a wrinkle: Though Maj. went for brevity, he eschewed all abbreviations, the word "dorm" included. "It's not a dorm, it's a dormitory. They're not kids; they're children." (Wonder what he thought of Maj.-short-for-Major?)

In a similar paradox, he saved pen strokes when Jack Peay checked out for regular dates with SuSu Smartt: "Destination: S^3."

Maj. believed that the only thing worse than a telephone was two telephones. A lover of music from hymns to operas, he disparaged two pianos at one time, or even two pianists on one bench. On a school trip to Nashville one January day, he passed by a tennis tournament on the television (not the TV) and remarked, "Little cold for tennis." On another trip down Interstate 59 to Birmingham with its sparse traffic, he observed, "Not sure why they built this road."

Bobby Dann recalls the discussion of a new post-military uniform code, and what constituted an appropriate shade of blue. "I'll never forget Maj.'s emphatic clarification of the rule in the words, 'Blue is blue!' "

And this one in countless repetitions: 'That was the rule and you broke it."

The pioneer recycler, he wrote every Please See Me ALB note on recycled paper, usually on the backs of mimeographed sheets or student rosters.

After 47 years the Burns family acquired their first color television set, a gift from daughter Helen. One Saturday Helen saw her father watching the baseball game of the week in black and white. A setting seemed to have shifted. When Helen asked him about the color, he said, "Nothing wrong with the television. I am just used to black and white."

A glowing cigarette ash might have been a minimal sign of a maximal grace. It was part of boarding students' mischief--"not theft, just a minor prank--to make a dark-of-night raid on the dining hall. Malcolm Colditz and four friends had a carefully orchestrated series of midnight raids on the cheese supply. Seven times it worked. "The eighth time," Colditz recounted, "as we approached the window, the cafeteria was black but there was a cigarette ash that seemed to illuminate the whole room. Maj. was there waiting for us. We were scared out of our wits at the glow of a cigarette 20 or 30 feet from where we were, and diverted immediately."

Did Maj. leave the cigarette burning as a warning--or was it accidental?

Those who knew him best can best answer.

KNOWING
he read your mind

"Maj. could smell a guilty man a mile away," observed Charlie Beard, and of course Beard knew because he had been one. Ned Watts passed the O.D. Room one day in his senior year on the way to get a Coke. "I heard the familiar, 'BOY!' and rolled down my sleeves and pulled up my tie as I turned into the office. Maj. met me at the door and said, 'Ned, some afternoon when you are dummy, see if you can find an extra picture of Bud [Burns Jr.] in his baseball uniform that I might have.'

"My mouth fell open and all I could say was 'Yes, Sir.' We thought no one knew of our secret bridge games in the publications office, behind double-locked doors and covered windows. We all should have known that Maj. knew every-thing and had a wonderful sense of what to do with that knowledge."

Turner Howard wasted no time in suffering his first infraction at school, brazenly thumbing his way to the tennis center in town, spending all afternoon and most of the night and then returning without checking in.

"When Maj. confronted me upon my arrival back at school, I quickly conjured every excuse imaginable in the time he allotted me. After I finally wound down (I knew I was in some kind of serious trouble; I could just look at him and sense that), he looked me straight in the eye, placed one hand on my shoulder and the other behind my head, and calmly replied: 'There's no excuse you can dream of that I haven't heard at one time or another during my 30 years here.' And you know, I believed the man. That was my first encounter with Maj. I never tried to wrangle my way out of anything at McCallie again--at least with him. It was a mystical encounter, not so much what he said as it was his presence, his experience."

For Bill Rogers the most unbelievable trait was Maj.'s ability to know what was going on with the boarding students.

"Most of the older students remember the drug store a short distance down from the old drill and track field--through the fence--where one could get a Coke or delicious milkshake. During my first year at McCallie I found myself campused. For some reason I convinced myself that I had to have one of those milkshakes. So, alone, I slipped through the fence, took the short walk down to the drugstore and had a shake and some crackers. I didn't see any known spies, students, or faculty, so naturally felt confident that my escapade had gone unnoticed.

"That evening at supper as The Maj. was checking each of us off his list, he asked me the simple question that immediately shook my little world and confidence.

"'Did you enjoy that milkshake?'

"CIA, FBI? I'll never know, but with his next breath he proved to be, as he usually was, judge, witness, and jury. 'That'll be two more weeks of E Class!'"

Social life at McCallie revolved around monthly formal dances. Date lists would be posted with names and addresses of the girls being mailed invitations. Each dance had a theme or spon- soring organization. For the Keo-Kio dance (a senior organization) Ed Henegar had no regular date, but as the president felt obligated to attend.

"As I checked out to go to the dance, Maj. sensed that I was conflicted about doing it. He got up from his desk and said, 'Come with me, Boy,' leaving those who were in line behind me standing there, and took me out of earshot. Evidently he sensed that my 'pious' conscience was conflicted about dancing, especially since the assembly speaker a few days earlier had delivered a stem-winding denunciation of worldly behaviors like smoking, drinking, and dancing, assuring us that those who did those things were in danger of perdition. Maj. said,

'You don't have to go to that dance if you don't think you should. But it will be all right with God if you do.' "

No teacher, no disciplinarian can be without error. Such a flawless record would distance him or her from very human students. And we can testify that at least twice Maj. missed it. Lyman Hodge had been up before the Discipline Committee regularly, so Maj. on the fourth go-round automatically put his name on the list. And this time, Hodge was squeaky-clean.

A Charlotte, N.C. alumnus invited Spencer III and Major Burns to stay in his home, and lost no time in expressing his gratitude to Maj. "I know you saw me [in a particular misdeed], but you acted as if you didn't, and for that I will always be grateful."

On the way home from Charlotte, but not before, Maj. turned to Spencer with doleful look and admitted,

"I never saw him."

PROJECTILES
pencils and erasers

This chapter might have been titled PENCILS.

Charles Stribling's memory comes with audio, the closest to profanity Maj. ever got. He can hear the familiar echo of Maj.'s "Dadgumit!' accompanied by the breaking of thrown pencils in the background.

On a rare occasion a boy got by with something, and Maj. himself acknowledged that "a large part of my fussing and screaming was aimed at myself--frustration because I wasn't getting across to them what I wanted to get across."

Case in point: Tom Divine came in late without penalty, seven whole minutes late. Maj. must have audited his records; days later he found the mistake and Divine received the Please See Me note. "I got the feeling that he was extremely frustrated that he couldn't give me 52 marks, which would have put me in E class. Seven, I hardly noticed. This is the only time in my McCallie career that Maj. threw a pencil at me."

The singular pencil was a rare thing. Ed Hurley tried to check out one Friday evening for a date. "I just did not have enough information to suit Maj. and he was throwing pencils and was downright mad. Then the phone rang. In an instant his voice changed as he answered with a ringing tenderness: 'McCallie School.' "

On her regular visits to the Burns graves in a Chattanooga cemetery, Bud Jr.'s widow Graham has often found not a spray of flowers, but a spray of pencils. This is a customary pilgrimage for a certain class on their reunion years, and their bouquet of pencils recalls the fact that Maj. was fond of lobbing a volley at them.

Perhaps ERASERS would be a gentler chapter title, and would also hit the mark. In class Maj. threw erasers, though by his own admission "I didn't throw nearly as many as I got credit for."

Hardwick Caldwell and a friend were on the back row in French class, causing some kind of commotion that merited the thrown eraser. It just might have been a source of youthful pride for Caldwell that he elicited that eraser.

In the 1972 school yearbook a full-page photograph of Maj.--the very one on the cover of this book--was in the Student section, preceding the other graduates. "It is particularly appropriate that Maj. Burns should be in this section among the students, because that is where Maj. Burns has always been. For 47 years he has been instructor, mother, nurse-maid and friend to literally thousands of McCallie students. If you have ever been before the Discipline Committee or looked forward to a French class, if you have come in late Friday night and been impaled on a flying pencil....you have known Maj."

HUMOR
good

During one particularly trying time--probably during many of those--Maj. advised Millie, "If you can just keep your sense of humor, you'll be all right." And Millie did.

ALB himself favored fun in the midst of trouble. In a newspaper interview he once explained, "Most of the fun is with the boys who give trouble. Not all, of course--but a lot of your pleasure comes from getting under the skin of someone who isn't trying hard enough." Humor, often subtle and sometimes puzzling at first, delivers such lessons well.

Buck Schimpf saved his skinny computer-generated grade reports from French II with numbers and comments in Maj.'s handwriting. Note the progression—or more accurately the regression.

October 15, 1965: EXAM 73, TERM 78

It's good to have Buck in my class. I am looking forward with pleasure to this year with him. I hope it proves profitable for him.

January 21, 1966: EXAM 63, TERM 71
Buck had a real close call. I am glad he made it. I want him to do much better. He is 27th of 29 in semester ranking.

March 4, 1966: EXAM 69, TERM 74
Buck needs to get himself out of the 70-75 danger zone.

April 22, 1966: EXAM 63, TERM 70
Buck is on terribly shaky ground. He needs to show marked improvement the rest of the year. I'll help him all I can.

May 23, 1966: EXAM 65, TERM 70
Buck made it, even if there was nothing to spare. I'm glad. He should say <u>au revoir</u> to French.

Haddon Allen was among the seniors who, shortly before graduation, rolled a teacher's Fiat "out of his car port on the Ridge to the front of the chapel in the middle of the night. There we carefully picked it up, front end first, then the back, to fit it perfectly in between the columns as we locked it up, windows closed. As the student body gathered for chapel that morning, the entrance was blocked, causing mild delay and a lot of laughs.

"As chapel started Dr. Spence put everyone on their honor to come forward if responsible. And of course, it took only a short while and we were all in chairs in front of Maj.'s office waiting to be disciplined. To make the point clearly, Maj. was busy in and out of his office and back and forth into Dr. Spence's office, and every time he passed us, under his breath he would say parts of the phrase, 'If you want to dance, you have to pay the fiddler.' On one trip it might be, 'if you want to dance...' and a few minutes later he'd come back by and softly say...'you got to pay the fiddler.' This went on for almost an hour before we were individually brought in to receive our sentence of the remaining weekends of school walking laps if we were not in Study Hall. But it was worth it."

Thorne Crosby described the Burnsian wit as the driest he has ever encountered, and confirmed that most cadets soon learned they'd never get the best of Major Burns in a battle of wits. It could happen almost anywhere. On a snowy night Crosby was returning to campus in the company of Charlie Battle, Joan Haley, Louis Field, Wendy Wiggins and his date Nancy Currey. On an icy road the car got in trouble at a turn. Injuries were minor though Crosby stayed in the Currey Clinic overnight.

"The next morning I called school and Major Burns answered the phone. Before I could tell my tale of woe, he started fussing at me for being AWOL. Finally I got the floor and began my story when Maj. interrupted.

" 'Boy, I know that. Battle and Field told me last night. Dr. Currey said you'd be released this morning. Can I send a car over to pick you up?' "

Rance Cleaveland was one of those boys who didn't give trouble, and was struck by Maj.'s sly and boy-friendly sense of humor.

"I recall having a brief conversation with him and a faculty member, probably when I was a tenth grader. I was an earnest kid, very deferential to adults (not a bad thing, of course, but not given to understanding that Adults Were People Too). Maj. was in his mid-seventies at the time and hence even more adult than the other teacher, so I was especially intimidated. Maj. said something that was obviously intended as teasing of the teacher, who laughed. I found myself laughing too, and this thought occurred to me then, probably for the first time: Major Burns is a person! And he's funny! In some sense I think of that as the starting point for my entry into adulthood. Of course, it still took some time. . . ."

The faculty loved this Maj. repartee. Spencer III recalls his father was fond of asking Maj., "Tell me why we don't have window fans in the dormitories?"

Maj.: "They suck all the air out and the boys could suffocate."

Dr. Spence: "Now, why shouldn't we fly on jets?"

Maj.: "You can look at a jet and tell it won't fly, because there are no propellers."

VACATION
singular, not plural

The ALB family vacation happened in the summer of 1952. It was a trip to Daytona Beach, Fla. He had just turned 50; Millie was 43; Bud was 15, and Helen was almost 6. Millie's mother, Helen Cooley, came along and was also the financial sponsor of the trip. This was the same year their 24-year residence in Douglas Hall ended with a move to a more spacious apartment in South Hutcheson Hall.

The family didn't have a car during most of the 1930s and 1940s. They took the Ridge Line of the electric streetcar or went places with friends who had cars. But around 1952 they became the proud owners of a used Pontiac. This is the chariot that ALB drove to Florida.

Helen remembers the first stop for gas. "I don't think we had gotten much past Ringgold and Maj. was already ready to turn back." But on they went to the beach, where Maj. was photographed doing typical tourist things, in shorts or swim trunks, like sitting under an umbrella on the beach and going into the ocean.

There was no other discussion in the Burns family about another family vacation, according to Helen. "We did it, we enjoyed it, and we checked if off our bucket list. Bud and I later joked that we felt sorry for friends who went on lots of vacations because they might have difficulty associating highlights with a particular trip. Not a problem for us!"

A summer off work is not necessarily a vacation. Maj. got the summer off once, but his only observance was to purchase a pair of Bermuda shorts. Not to wear, just to purchase.

A vacation is quite different from a trip to get from Point A to Point B, and if that process involved a train, Maj. was all over it. He loved trains. While at Emory, he rode the train to and from Atlanta. The tracks ran close to his East Chattanooga neighborhood, so his family would hear the train whistle and leave by car to greet him at the station.

He noted that Meigs County was the only Tennessee county that didn't have a railroad, a bit of trivia he and Helen enjoyed. Father and daughter went on a rail excursion to Huntsville, Ala. not long before his death. While he had slowed down physically by then, he still navigated steadily and youthfully between the cars.

TRIP
of a lifetime

There was only one vacation of this family's lifetime, but then there was the trip of a lifetime for ALB and Millie.

The Class of 1961 thought it up, and that summer the trip of a lifetime happened. That senior class, instead of a class gift to the school, surprised the Burnses with a trip to Europe. For months the boys dropped their nickels, dimes and more into the box, often adding checks sent from a relative back home. Then alumni joined in to make the trip a first-class, two-week adventure. Maj. admitted that "from a selfish standpoint, this is my fondest memory of the school."

It is likely that his delight in this gift was anything but selfish, but came from the knowledge that it equally honored Millie's years of selfless service on campus, particularly her constant sharing of husband and father. C. M. S. McIlwaine, his friend and colleague, and also a legend at McCallie, wrote in the alumni journal that "no McCallie man has ever received as fine a token of affection or deserved it more." Larry Gold of that giving class says that naming his best memory is easy: the day they surprised the Burnses with their trip.

"What an assembly that was!

"A few of us knew in advance that this was happening. Major Burns had a habit of standing in the back of the chapel to catch late-comers. He would wait until the last minute and then march down the center aisle with his long arms spread wide like some ungainly heron, snaring any students so tardy that they tried to sneak under those arms. Of course, it was to no avail. That day was no different.

"But, when he got to the front and came up onto the stage, there was Dr. Spence with an empty suitcase and an envelope and Major Burns looked flustered and confused, for just a moment. Then, when Dr. Spence made the presentation and Millie came out from the back of the stage, it was just too much! I had never, ever seen Major Burns at a loss for words, but he was totally flummoxed and could not speak. Of course, all the boys and faculty gave him and Millie a standing ovation and everyone yelled and screamed. I can still see it."

Maj. here picks up with his report to the ones who started it all. The two-page letter that arrived in the home mailbox of each class member reveals the rich relationship between

144

givers and recipients; the conversation begun in their late childhood was to last a lifetime.

To: Members of McCallie Class of 1961
Subject: Whereabouts of ALB, August 6-30, 1961
September 20, 1961

"The trip to Europe is an accomplished fact, and I can prove it, if necessary, with receipted hotel bills, airplane and boat coupons, and suchlike. It was absolutely wonderful from start to finish, and I want to give you a general idea of what happened. Remember, I warned you at the senior banquet that I was going to work up a report and circulate it. Well, here goes!

"On Saturday night, August fifth at 10:00 I walked out of the O.D. Room, leaving behind a clean desk (hard to believe?) and with all necessary records in the possession of Mr. James, who was kind enough to do my work during the last week of summer school. A little after two the next day, Sunday, August sixth, we left for the airport with a police escort, red light turning on top of car and at a rapid clip. You can see the advantage of being an old friend of the Commissioner of Police. Soon after we arrived at the airport, quite a good-sized crowd began to show up, composed mainly of McCallie teachers and staff members and their families. When Mrs. Burns and I started through the gate to go to the plane, several in the group began to throw rice at us. I didn't get it out of my hair for some time.

"We found two seats next to a young man, but he very gallantly moved, saying that that would give us more privacy. After 33 years!

"We arrived in New York about 8:00 and went to the St. Regis Hotel where we were the guests of an old McCallie boy for nearly three days. Two other old friends, also old McCallie boys, took us over until boat time the following Wednesday. Monday night we had dinner at the Algonquin, saw 'Mary, Mary' and ended up at Sardi's. The following night, dinner was at Trader Vic's, the show was 'Carnival' and we closed things up at the penthouse apartment of one of them with a big gabfest, living over some wonderful days in the early 1940s.

"Came Wednesday and time to board the Queen Elizabeth. The feat was accomplished without incident, and we set sail at five o'clock in the afternoon. We missed the Statue of Liberty when we went below to put up our life-jackets after a lifeboat drill. I think I had mine on wrong. Life on board the ship was nothing short of wonderful. The accommodations were even better than I had imagined, the sea air was bracing, and the food out of this world. I am sure that I have never spent five days that were any more enjoyable or restful.

"On Monday August 14 we landed at Cherbourg and rode the boat-train to Paris, where we arrived in the late afternoon. We went directly from the station to the Claridge Hotel where we were to spend one of the big weeks of our lives. It is quite a place, the Claridge, situated as it is on the Champs-Elysees, no less, quite near the breathtaking Arc de Triomphe. You didn't stop short of the best, either in Paris or London. The next day we started seeing the sights of Paris, and you had better believe that they are there. Morning and afternoon tours brought to our eyes places that we had always heard about and seen pictures of, but seeing them at first-hand is very different. There were many times when we were thrilled almost beyond expression. I think we made nearly every well-known place in Paris, including the sidewalk cafes, the Lido, and the Folies. Some day I might whisper to you just where our seats turned out to be at the Folies. But why wait?

"They were on the first row. I pledge you I didn't buy them there; it just happened that way. We ended up the week by having dinner at La Tour d'Argent. The experience almost defies description. It apparently is one of the fine restaurants of the world, and we ate at a table right at a window, through which we could look down on the Seine and see Notre-Dame Cathedral, floodlighted in the background. It was an experience we will never forget. The food wouldn't have had to be good to make the experience memorable, but it was delicious.

"I heard a lot of French and found that my special brand was adequate. In fact, a taxi driver with whom I was talking said I spoke *tres bien*. I think, though, he just wanted a bigger tip.

"And now to London on August 21. We flew across the English Channel on British European

Airways. It took only an hour. In London, where we were to spend nine more days, brimful of excitement and pleasure, we stayed at the Westbury Hotel, a new American place. It had a different atmosphere from that of the Claridge in Paris, but it was swanky, too. Sightseeing in London took about the same form as in Paris. On numerous tours, we saw Westminster Abbey, St. Paul's Cathedral, the Houses of Parliament, the Tower of London and many other spots, all of which gave us a tremendous charge. One day we had an all-day trip to Oxford and Stratford-upon-Avon, which was most enjoyable and satisfying. Trips through Warwick Castle and Windsor Castle were great.

"Since all good things have to end, August 30 came around and we made our way to the London Airport to board Pan-American's jet flight 101. There is nothing to this jet-flight travel. You just get on, settle down, eat lunch, have tea, and then you are in New York. Seriously, I can hardly believe that the time for crossing the Atlantic on one of the world's fastest ships is five days and that the jet did it in just under seven hours. That's moving. After clearing customs at Idlewild, we taxied over to LaGuardia, hopped a United flight and arrived in Chattanooga at 7:50 Wednesday night, August 30: 3800 miles in a little over 12 hours!

"Well, that's it, but it is a sorry summary of one of the finest experiences that ever happened to any man. This thing was perfectly planned and moved like clockwork. The whole affair was nothing short of fantastic, and it seems too wonderful ever to have happened. Did I just dream up the whole thing? No, it was real, and the marvelous things that we enjoyed as a result of your thoughtfulness, kindness and generosity will give us unspeakable joy and satisfaction the rest of out lives. I didn't deserve it, and I know it, but I am so happy and grateful that it all came about. Thank you--from the bottom of my heart, thank you.

"And now another year has started at McCallie, number thirty-seven for me, and, as usual, I am hoping that it is going to be the best one yet. There is a bunch of new boys around and seven new teachers. The year is nearly two weeks old now, and so far things have been very smooth. There is only one thing wrong, and that is the fact that a lot of familiar faces are missing. As I walk down the halls, pass through the Study Halls, stroll through the dormitories, work the cafeteria lunch, and roam the campus, things don't seem quite right without all of you around. But I really wouldn't have it otherwise, because the time has come for you to move on to something new and to commit yourselves to still more opportunities and challenge as you prepare for the life that stretches out ahead of you. As you begin your college careers, my very best wishes are with you. Give to this new phase of your lives the best that you have; being who you are, you cannot do less.

"Thank you again for your part in our wonderful, fantastic trip. But most of all thank you for all you have meant to ·me and for giving me the privilege of being your friend. Mrs. Burns joins me in affectionate regards.

"Most sincerely, Arthur L. Burns"

Can you imagine the long list of givers of coins, writers of checks, planners of exquisite details-- grateful boys and their families who made possible an adventure of this magnitude?

At the airport, "quite a good-sized crowd began to show up."

FAMILIES
overlapping circles

In thinking of ALB's influence, Graham Burns shook her head and marveled: "There are so many overlapping circles here."

Although former head Spencer III declares with surety that Maj. would have become the man he was in any environment, this school was just as surely the best place for him. Yes he was trustworthy, but not all trustworthy people are granted such complete trust.

The family circles began in homes on the side of the Ridge on the land once farmed by Dr. T. H. McCallie. Here were the founders' and head-masters' homes of Park, Spence, Bob, Spencer III, and Dr. Park's daughter, Miss Anne McCallie, who worked with alumni.

Day students went home to their families each night. But the school still pulsed with boarding life 24 hours a day. In Douglas Hall, Founder's Home, Maclellan and Belk Halls and in South

151

and North Hutcheson Halls during the Burns tenure, a life around the clock was sustained by the teachers who raised their own families in apartments in the dormitories on campus.

Millie coveted their private family time and often prepared Sunday meals for the four of them at home. But on some weeknights at the dining hall, where faculty and their families took meals at long wooden tables with boys, they presided over their own table. A boy who managed a seat at that table did not forget it. Robert Hovis was one of those. Thirty-five years after graduation, he still anchored himself keenly to the memory of the teacher he called "Bud privately or Mr. Burns in public. I was privileged to sit at his table in the dining hall, on the west side, about the center."

After these dining hall meals Millie and Maj. strolled home holding hands, to the great embarrassment of their adolescent daughter. Inevitably there came the knock on the door, the phone call about problems on campus or back at a boy's home. Then, with homework begun for Bud Jr. and Helen, Maj. went back to the O.D. Room, tending to Study Hall and the expected emergencies. He was known to have shown up among the boys one 3 a.m., his suit over his pajamas, seeking answers.

The Burns home wasn't just a haven for the Burns family. Jim McCallie, son of Dr. Bob McCallie, found a second home there.

"My fondest memories are the countless hours spent with Bud Jr. playing APBA basketball in the Burnses' South Hutcheson Hall apartment while Maj. and Millie entertained over coffee in the kitchen. This is the same apartment where we later lived with our girls Mary Claire and Laura. The gracious ease and kindness of Maj. and Millie and their unpretentious welcome and acceptance of this young boy and eventually teenager into their home, at all hours of the day and evening, gave me an incredible home away from home with my brother Bud. Nancy and I continue our proud relationship with the Burns family as the godparents of one of the Burns grandchildren, Graham."

A glimpse into the realities of their home life widens the lens of appreciation for both Burnses. Richard Park grew up near campus.

"Maj. and Millie were dear to me, and I loved them as second parents. They were easy, and they were fun. By easy, I mean that they never bothered Bud and me. They left us alone to do our thing. I would like to think it was because we were ideal children and needed no supervision. More realistically, knowing them, I bet they had their antennas focused on us without any awareness on our part."

Yes, Maj. was an expert at that antenna thing.

"By fun, I mean I thoroughly enjoyed being in their presence. I would enter the Burns home via the kitchen door at Hutcheson Hall, often to find them sitting at the little table in the kitchen enjoying a second cup of coffee. There was no pretense in the Burns household. They had little as measured by material objects. But they possessed much in terms of enjoying the simple pleasures of life, while at the same time having such a major impact on the lives of countless young men."

The faculty received the same welcome and acceptance. Steve Bartlett was mentored by Maj. as a fledgling teacher. This he recalls:

"As a newbie, I was assigned to do periodic night Study Hall duty, and was a floor man, patrolling among the C class and below boys and serving as a runner. At 7:00 p.m. the desk man would take the roll and note the attendance on a sheet, which I would then take down to Maj.'s office in Caldwell Hall. Maj. would look the sheet over and attempt to reconcile any absences by checking who was in the Infirmary and who might be otherwise excused. Then he would send me back up-stairs. When the second half of Study Hall began at 8:20, I again would take the list down to Maj., who was patiently waiting in his office to check it over. I recall his kindness and patience with me as a complete rookie, to McCallie as well as to the faculty. He helped me to think that I might just make it at this unique school. As I headed back up the stairs, Maj. was putting on his topcoat and hat, preparing to head home, past the flagpole and Alumni Hall and over to his house on Kyle Street."

Michael Bailey was awfully young when he started teaching, and later as an administrator could sympathize with Maj.'s dilemma. "Maj. had a hard job with young teachers. You want to support them but you know they are going too far, or reporting something that shouldn't be reported. He managed to take care of those things without letting a new teacher feel like an idiot. He didn't correct us. He probably told the boy, 'Mr. Bailey reported this and I'm sorry he did. But let's just act like I gave you a terrible punishment.'"

***

On weekends faculty children roamed the campus among friends in what Bud, Jr. described as the most wonderful childhood he could imagine, "with heroes right and left." Maj. circled from home and back again all weekend, checking boys out with appropriate suspicion and then safely back in, with fatherly relief.

Sam Dougherty was a McCallie student at the same time that his mother, Naomi Dougherty, was the headmasters' secretary. He was therefore a close-up observer of the overlapping circles of family life at McCallie. The mother observed to her son that the McCallie family-- that is, those who were actual McCallie kin-- "had a way about them that gave all the McCallie faculty and staff a sense of belonging and being part of a greater family of the school." In the extended family centered around the school's founders, and later co-headmasters Drs. Spence and Bob McCallie, and the associate headmasters, Sam Dougherty affirmed that Maj.

stood as the "unmistakable Patriarch of the Long Blue Line of us McCallie Boys."

The McCallie family that led the school had complete trust in the constant care Burns took with the boys. Dougherty remembers his mother's describing Maj.'s "perfect work ethic, everything always done and on time, unspeakable precision, a steadfastness and constancy in the day-to-day operations of McCallie. There was simply no one else like him." Utterly trustworthy in his legendary thoroughness, Maj. left no concerns unnoticed, no business with the boys unfinished. Spencer III could speak for more than one of the McCallie family headmasters that "we didn't know what he was doing. He handled different things with kids--my father and Dr. Park didn't know--of course they didn't! They didn't need to. He solved problems and he was always respectful."

Those family circles overlapped so well that, as headmaster Robert Kirk Walker famously stated, "The Long Blue Line Sometimes Forms a Circle."

Linda Snodgrass, wife of Maj.'s student and McCallie colleague, understood this circle well when she fell in love with Ed.

'When I first met Edward in graduate school at Duke, I knew immediately about McCallie. I don't remember when I finally learned about where he went to college, as that seemed purely superfluous. He talked often about Major Burns and his influence on his life. Edward's heart's

156

desire was to return to McCallie and to be able to give the kind of encouragement and support to boys that he had received at McCallie.

"After we became engaged, we drove to Chattanooga to announce the formal engagement. When we drove into town, we drove directly to McCallie and to the Burns house. Major Burns was the first McCallie person I met. We went, because Edward wanted Major Burns' approval. About 13 years later, after Edward and I moved to campus, we lived in Major Burns' house. Edward had come full circle!"

TECHNIQUE
straight and straight

In dealing with his students, Andy Smith, as a teacher of architecture, still asks himself, "What would Maj. do?" And thus Maj.'s influence, at times both easy and impossible to quantify, continues to shape relationships between teacher and student.

The recollections of Franklin McCallie, grandson of Professor Spencer McCallie Sr., and son of headmaster Spencer Jr., redound around Burns' powerful shaping influence of Franklin's teaching and administrative career as principal of Kirkwood High School, a large public school in the St. Louis suburb of Kirkwood, Mo.

Three little words, "Straight and straight!" verbalized a kind of mysterious technique for minimalist Burns. The following is straight (and straight) from Principal McCallie, who remembers that "One of Maj.'s favorite instructions-- possibly better called an 'edict'--was always on my tongue, and I never had to explain it to any student.

"When a McCallie student asked Maj. if he could go anywhere that proved out of the ordinary, his response was a bare bones: 'Straight and straight, Boy.'

"No one at McCallie ever had to ask Maj. what 'straight and straight' meant, and no one at Kirkwood High School ever had to ask me either. And woe to the student who wandered.

"By the time I was a child, living in a faculty apartment in Founder's Home, Maj. was already legend, and he had many more years to serve. Few educators build the level of respect that Maj. fostered. I often saw the effects of this respect, and was moved by both that respect and the manner in which it helped Maj. do a better job.

"McCallie's campus was smaller then, but still something over 40 acres. Day or night, students liked to skip campus when they could.

"I was in Major Burns' presence several times when I saw him look as far as several hundred yards to where a student or students were plan-ning to attempt their break-out from campus. Most teachers and/or administrators would have several choices: yell, run after them, chase them by car, check the record of absentees for that time period for possible names, or allow this one to pass in favor of getting them next time.

"Maj. chose an effective alternative, much less used by most educators. He would look straight at the escapees, regardless of recognition or not (however, one of his great talents was recognizing any student, anywhere!), and after getting eye contact--because students who were skipping campus would always look back to see if an adult were watching--Maj. would merely stand and shake his head 'NO.' Each time--regardless of distance--those students would return the way they had come. I never saw Maj. fail in this manner.

"Once I slipped out of Study Hall early and was stealthily making my way to the school cafeteria to beat the lunch line, Maj. worked his magic on me--from 100 yards. I took that lesson to heart.

"Some years later, I was named principal of Kirkwood High School. I found myself modeling Major Burns as often as I could. I knew, of course, that a mainstay of his educational phil-osophy was to trust and respect his students, and I hoped that if I genuinely gave that trust and respect, it might as genuinely be returned.

"The day came when I was put to the test, and I, in turn, put Maj.'s method to the test. I was leading a tour of our Mothers' Club. We were at one end of the campus with a 200-yard walkway between us and four students who were sneaking--as nonchalantly as possible--toward the parking lot at the other end of campus. Lunch was two hours ahead, so these students were not where they were supposed to be. I could not in good conscience let them go, but I also could not do a 200-yard dash in front of these moms. Nor could I yell at the top of my lungs in their presence.

"The solution was instinctive. I looked full at them, saw that I had their attention, and then slowly shook my head 'No.' The students took several seconds to consider their situation, and then returned to the building from whence they had come. I knew this retreat would be final; the students had no place else to go but where they were supposed to be.

"All members of the Mothers' Club tour had seen this interaction. Thirty moms turned to me and said, almost in unison, 'I don't believe what I just saw. How did you do that?'

" 'Maj. taught me.'

"And we continued our tour.

"There were other ways that I imitated Maj. I often thought of Maj. when I walked the halls and spoke to every student I could, nodding when I couldn't speak for one reason or the other, but invariably giving recognition.

"If Maj. trusted, had faith in, and loved his students, he also understood his role as keeper of the rules. Maj. knew very well that certain students were going to test the system. So how did a great educator who had faith in his students hold to that trust and still look out for breaks in the line? He verbalized clearly what he wanted; he believed that each student would comply, and knew he still had to be observant for those students who invariably might not be able to keep to the straight and straight."

Today we are old and we are young.
         We are short and we are tall.
         We have long hair, and short hair, and no hair.
         We are different, and many...
But all of us are richer in love, in faith, in hope,
         because our paths crossed yours,
         and you walked a few important steps with us
                  in the path of
                           our growing up.
                                    ...And you loved us.

Maj, we are grateful to God for you.
We love you.

         ...Your loyal sons are we.

                                    James H. Daughdrill, Jr.
                                    '52

This assessment is a portion
of the typewritten poem a former student
sent ALB at retirement.

164

ASSESSMENT
but not canonization

Recognition came regularly to ALB. Yearbooks in the early decades often named him Best Teacher, Most Popular, or Best Dressed (maybe second place for that). The 1937 and 1951 yearbooks were dedicated to him. In 1976 the Burns Student Center opened in the new academic building. In 1978 Lockett Lodge was renovated and refurnished in memory of ALB. That initiative was led by Jim Talley and the Class of 1942. In 2010 a new dormitory was dedicated: Burns Hall. Funding for that monument came mostly from Paddy & Dan Blalock '49, Andrea & Jim Burns '89, Betsy & Hardwick Caldwell '40, Kitty & Hacker Caldwell '66, Suzanne & Kirk Crawford '77, Mary Anne & Alan Dickson '49, Francie & Tom Fanjoy '50, India & Greg Keith '74, Joanie & Ed Michaels '60, Norma & Olan Mills II '48, Nancy & David Stonecipher '59, The Dickson Foundation, the B.C. Moore Foundation, and the StoneyPeak Foundation.

Student, colleague, employer, parent and alumni saw the man from five aligned perspectives.

At Maj.'s death Greg Hullender realized he was in the McCallie class of important endings and beginnings.

"In many ways the class of 1977 seems to have consisted of beginnings and ends. My first year at McCallie was the first year without Dr. Park McCallie and Sack Milligan. It was also Major Burns' last year as Dean of Students. During my six years Dr. Spence retired, the last class that had been under the military graduated, a new football stadium was built and McCallie moved from the old buildings into a spectacular new complex. And now you tell me that Major Burns has gone too.

"I am going to believe that the student body behaved well while Maj. lay in state in the chapel. They probably didn't know him very well, but I want to believe that even today McCallie students can be reverent at a great man's passing."

Hullender's analysis calls to mind the words of Plato, that we are to bequeath to our children "not riches but the spirit of reverence." Maj., having none of the former, had plenty to share of the latter.

Charles Stribling Sr. became president of Missouri Military Academy, but his first school job was at McCallie when he was fresh out of college. "I was assigned dormitory duty in

Founder's Home and received tutelage in this art from Major Burns. As he was with his students, he was very patient and kind with this neophyte instructor, at the same time displaying the example of rectitude for which he was known."

Professor Spencer McCallie told daughter Mary McCallie Ware, around 1940, "I could get another French teacher, but I could never get another Arthur Lee Burns. I consider him the greatest dormitory man in the country." She knew he meant by that term Maj.'s responsibility for all boarding students, and she added that "disciplinarians are rarely loved but he was. My husband said he thought it was because he played no favorites, was absolutely fair and the boys knew he was genuinely concerned about their welfare."

Speaking from a father's perspective, Horace Coward of Goldsboro, N.C., wrote Maj. in appreciation for "everything you did for [my son] Lee. The only criticism I would make of the school is that Maj. Burns has to work too much--which is none of my business!"

Burns was, however, not all work and no play, but often playful at work.

Goodbye Mr. Chips was a popular book in the 1930s and a movie in two versions (1939 and 1969). Chips was a teacher at a boys' boarding school. Maj. came to be identified with this fictional educator, described by author James Hilton as receiving "the best reward of a well-spent life: to grow old beloved." The comparison even made the local papers, to the dismay of Fielder Cook who was directing movies in Hollywood. Cook was at the same time one of Maj.'s most loyal correspondents, writing his mentor in a distinctive backhand script with California postmark.

"I must protest the identification of you with the 'Mr. Chips' myth. He was OK. But you are something more special and a lot more human. Mr. Chips was a loner, a lonely man who had nothing but his service to his school. You have all the passion of A Very Rich Heart to give and everyone benefited--school as well as students. You had the toughness of life as well as its sensitivity, and we should not overlook that outrageous humor and confounding rage toward the hypocrisy of life.

"There is a lot to be said for the Fun, the Sneaky, the Rebellious, and the Dissatisfied. I would not like to see you canonized."

The following exchange reported by teacher Michael Bailey might hint that no canonization is necessary--but you'll have to separate wit from seriousness to uncover the truth in it.

Student XYZ was a rascal, but he could be polite too. Once his mother visited, and outside the freshman dormitory, XYZ said, "Mr. Bailey, I would like for you to meet my mother."

Bailey looked startled. "Why, XYZ, you did not tell me you had parents!"

His mother, who had tolerated his antics from birth, took no offense, but ruefully agreed. "I know what you mean."

For four years XYZ terrorized the faculty with insolence and impudence. Teacher after teacher would turn his offenses over to ALB. The next day they would learn no punishment had been decreed. It seems ALB had determined the violations were of the spirit of the rules and not the letter.

At graduation XYZ misbehaved egregiously but escaped with diploma in hand. After the ceremony, ALB was in Caldwell Hall. Michael Bailey said, "He set me up. We were the only two in the building. I entered the Millis-Evans Room, and Maj. was beating his head against the wall.

" 'What's wrong, Maj.?'

"Maj. said, 'I have seen the error of my ways.'

" 'What do you mean?'

" 'What I mean is, XYZ is NOT worth a darn!'"

***

Jim Greenwalt returned to campus to visit with his old teachers, Mr. Mac (McIlwaine) and Maj. "Maj. and I talked sitting on the steps of the administration building not too long before his passing. He talked with me as if he remembered me even as a seventh grader. I don't believe that anything ever escaped his memory. He even recalled that he found me dangling by my topcoat from a coat hook in the O.D. Room as a seventh grader, courtesy of Bill Donelson."

FAREWELLS
endings
without loose ends

The academic calendar forces regular wel-
comes and farewells. Every September in those
days, teachers were called on when parents
said good-bye to their sons and settled them in
Spartan dormitories, far from the comforts of
home and Mama. ALB was not one who liked
farewells, but he was adept at helping families
through the transition.

On the long car ride up from Clarksdale, Miss.,
E'Lane Bobo rehearsed the good-bye to son Bob
Jr. "We were sick, sick, sick. I just couldn't believe
we were going to leave him there for someone
else to raise. Our schools here were in
shambles and we had felt this was the best for
him. It was Maj. that reassured us, told us what
a wise thing we were doing and how much it
would mean to our son. In fact, I remember his
exact words: 'A parent has to love a child a lot
to send him off to school.' "

171

For ALB it may have been easier to teach someone how to manage than to take one's own turn at farewells.

The last rites of June included the image of Maj. walking slowly home through a deserted campus, weary, and somehow its import caught the eyes of two young teachers. Spencer McCallie III noticed it first. He was sitting outside the west door of his Founder's Home apartment when Maj. walked by. "Graduation is over, it's hot outside but he has on his coat and hat. He is walking slowly. I am thinking that he is thinking too, 'I'll probably never see some of them again. It's done and they are all happy, going off without a backward glance, and they think they won't miss us.'"

The teachers knew better.

The next year English teacher George Hazard knocked on Spencer's door at school's end. "I want to sit in your yard and watch Maj. come by." Together they sat on a bench outside, and sure enough, Spencer reported, "30 minutes later we look down by the flagpole and he has on the fedora and the coat, kind of bent, must be exhausted. He is walking slowly because he is so sad. This says it all. Hazard and I are taking it in. It's the grandfather who will never see them again."

Maj. was a man who left no loose ends.

His final assembly before retirement was a normal, end-of-the-year assembly. This is how it happens at school. Finality sneaks up on you: the last moment of the last visit, or game, or class, or assembly. Or career.

Dean Warren James recounted it. "Through all the verbiage some less-than-interested junior on the front row of the balcony had been occasionally dipping the little ring-contraption into a liquid and blowing bubbles on the ones below.

"Major Burns finally came to the microphone with his usual handful of announcements. First there was a list of people who had overdue library books; then there was a list of those who still owed him laps on the bullring. Next he reminded everyone of the mandatory attendance at Class Day. Then, of course, his familiar list of those he just had to see. . . .

"When he stopped and turned to leave, it happened. There was first just a hesitant scattering of applause. Others took it up quickly, the bubbles stopped, and in seconds all the boys were on their feet in a spontaneous and thunderous ovation of love for a man who had just told them they had to walk the bullring. Faculty on stage stood and joined in; the backstage crew came out to become a part of it. Something had come to an end and the students realized the drama of the moment.

"Maj. turned to take the applause."

His eventual farewell to the school was protracted until the day it was impossible to ignore. In 1972 Maj. retired at the obligatory 70; however, the Burnses remained in their campus home and he was still present daily on campus. "I miss it," he admitted, "but it's a good miss." In a three-page handwritten letter to Irwin Hyatt when he was "going on my fifth year of relief from responsibilities", ALB finally got around to reporting about himself on page three. "I have been made to feel welcome on the campus and I go over every morning to help with the mail and keep in touch that way and by wandering around talking with old and new friends among the faculty and boys. I am having a happy life. I am so thankful for so much. God has been very good to me."

In this same correspondence Hyatt, a professor at Emory University, spoke of writing a book, *Our Ordered Lives Confess*, a copy of which he had sent to Maj. "Whatever merits this book may have are due to an unusual degree to the years I spent at McCallie in the 1950s. I think [there] I acquired at least some appreciation of how the English language ought to be written, and more importantly, from the example of people like you, an appreciation of the fact that fine teachers who influence young people are that way more because of what they are than what they say."

We are to understand, then, that the life, not mere words, transfers the lessons.

One October day, not too many months after these letters, Burns stuck his head in the headmaster's office then occupied by Spencer

McCallie III. "I just wanted to tell you, and I don't know why I want to tell you, but I am going into the hospital for some foot surgery."

Spencer didn't then realize the momentousness of that stop. "I was busy with many inconsequential things--and he was dead within a week."

Here is one unknown. "The thing I don't know," Spencer mused, "is what happened when we had to let a boy go. (Maj. was after all the longtime head of the Discipline Committee.) You had to let them go because if you didn't, other boys would get on the wrong track. I'm sure he was very sad, though I never heard him say." And perhaps that silence said exactly what Spencer suspected.

First and last, Maj. shaped McCallie for Ronnie Thomas.

"I came in the summer of 1962. I was 13 years old. The first person I met from McCallie's staff was Maj. God knew what I needed and Maj. delivered the message." In the years to come, Maj. became like Ronnie's father.

"After graduation, the last thing I did was hug Maj., then looked back and said 'Thank you God and bless my earthly father, Major Arthur Lee Burns.'"

Their last conversation was by phone, on the final day of October in 1977, the day before Maj.'s death.

Maj. was present in the milestones.

At times Maj. <u>was</u> the milestone.

RETIRED

presently and gracefully

Maj. retired with a very present grace. Down through the decades his alarm was always set at 4:45. He would dress in coat and tie, go over to check on the school and come back to fix the family breakfast. Not so in retirement, when he pushed the hands of the alarm clock all the way up to 5:00 a.m. Still not a family that rushed things.

As he explained in print to the school's scattered alumni:

"My McCallie experience of 47 years had its beginning in September of 1925, and it ran without interruption until midnight last August 31, when my contract for 1971-72 expired. The event was not highlighted by any dramatic incident or deep thoughts. I didn't wake up moaning, 'What will I do with my time?' I didn't wake up leaping and shouting for joy to be rid of the job. As a matter of fact, I didn't wake up at all. There was neither any feeling of elation or

177

depression. I had gone to bed about 10 o'clock, and I slept through the alarm.

"My life is different now, but it is still a good one. I come over to the campus every morning and say hello to a lot of old friends and try to make some new ones among the boys who have come to McCallie this year for the first time. Then help the ladies in the Bursar's office with the mail, after which I go home to rest. I usually make a second trip over in the afternoon. The headmaster has been kind enough to invite me to come over whenever I want to and to stay as long as I please. He didn't tell me to keep my mouth shut about school matters, but I do. I don't express any opinions unless I am asked. And nobody much asks.

"My years at McCallie began with seven other new teachers. Their names I shall never forget: Dunlap, McIlwaine, Purdy, Hill, Boggs, McMillan, and Marion. Ralph Boggs, Francis McMillan and Jack Marion left at the end of the first year for other fields. Gene Hill stayed on for nearly 10 years when he entered the textile field. That left the 'four horsemen', Dunlap, McIlwaine, Purdy, and Burns. Without bragging and admitting to many shortcomings, that was a pretty special bunch. Our relationship represents one of my great privileges. Purdy left us in the 1950s and now Dunlap and I bow out leaving Mac, the baby of the group, to carry on.

"As I have looked back, I have marveled at the abilities that Doctor and Professor put into play, not only to run a good school but to be everlastingly at work to make it better, and it was all done on income from tuition. To bring it through the days of the Depression was an almost superhuman feat. I am grateful to my parents who made it possible for me to spend four years here as a student from 1916 to 1920. And I owe a great debt of gratitude to my wife and two children for their tolerance and forbearance as they shared me, sometimes extravagantly, with McCallie as I attempted to carry on my work in the way that I thought I had to do it. My wife, especially, deserves a big share in any credits that might have come my way.

"Of course, my debt to Doctor and Professor McCallie beggars expression. They were giants and yet they were always fair and understanding. I'm afraid I never got over being scared of them. A call from one of their offices, 'Burns, I would like to see you,' always put all my defense machinery in operation until the interview was over.

"It was Professor who, one night when I was a senior, said something to me that was a milestone in my life. It was during the summer, and for some reason there was a watermelon cutting on the campus and I was present. Somewhat out of the blue he said to me, 'Burns, when you are about to finish college and think you might want to come back to McCallie to teach, get in touch with me.' I never forgot the kind invitation, but I'm not sure I took it seriously either. There came a time, though, when I didn't know what I was going to do with my life, when I took some action. I'm convinced the Lord had a lot to do with it. I wrote for an appointment, talked to Professor and Doctor and Dr. Woods, and signed a contract. That started it and turning 70 stopped it.

"Dr. Woods (T.E.P.) meant a very great deal to me, as did Tommy (Dr. R. F.) Thomason and many others. On Professor's death and Doctor's retirement as headmaster, Spence and Bob and Bill Pressly took over and furnished strong leadership to the school. Bill Pressly resigned to go to take over what was to become the Westminster Schools in Atlanta. Bob's sudden death in 1965 was a staggering blow, but Spence assumed the full responsibility and has done a fine work. I am grateful to all of them for putting up with my sometimes-sorry efforts. I owe so much to so many.

"But in a real way I am a debtor chiefly to the 3500 boys that I have seen graduate from this school and for many more who for one reason or another didn't stay until they finished. They are the ones who have meant the most to me and who have given me a satisfaction, happiness, and joy that I could never give expression to. I failed them so many times, but they were always understanding about my frailties and shortcomings, and I love them for it and for their many other qualities. I was guilty of a lot of bungling in my approach to my responsibilities, but I like to think that I always meant well. Most of the time, I want to think, I got credit for trying. I had no particular technique. I guess my good friend Jim Daughdrill has sized me up about right in a poem he has written about me. He says that I walked a few steps along the road with boys as they were growing up. I hope I have.

"Just one serious note now and I'll be through. I want to testify, as I close out my time at McCallie, to my complete faith in the McCallie of tomorrow. Great things are in prospect for the physical development of the school, but more important, I have every confidence that the McCallie of the future will be built on the solid foundation of faith in God and in his son Jesus Christ and on the principles of honor, honesty, and integrity which have always made McCallie, McCallie."

As the McCallie of the future took shape in the post-Burns years, Spencer III looked through the school's financial records and thought of conversations with his father and other heads of independent schools in the South. Many of those schools had closed their doors, Spencer realized.

What had kept McCallie alive?

He went back to the budgets of lean years past. He realized the generous commitment of faculty despite small salaries, bare-bones facilities and school-wide belt-tightening. He discovered a record of the retirement income his father received, sparse because there were no retirement plans. And he had his answer for what had kept McCallie alive and healthy. Knowing this, that those who served there had made it happen together. Spencer's eyes filled with tears.

Bob Franklin, whose student days were during Maj.'s on-campus retirement, has a framed picture of ALB in his Signal Mountain home. When Franklin me his daughter recently at a civic function, the McCallie connection was established, and he said, "Yes, I knew your father. In fact I spoke to him this morning."

What?

"When I pass his picture on my bookshelf, I often speak to him. 'Hello, Maj.'"

George Farrell noted at his 50th class reunion that "I think about Maj. almost every day."

GRANDDADDY
bearing Cracker Jacks

Grandfatherhood may have eased Maj.'s transition from full-time to retired-time. He doted on his five grandchildren, so conspicuously that Georgiana Webb described as a favorite memory, "the special look on his face when he looked at one of his grandchildren." Bud Jr. and Graham had seven in all: Carol, his namesake Lee (ALB III), Jim, Graham, Lucy, Edy and May. Edy and May were born after Maj.'s death, but they can still tell the stories.

Carol had a decade with her grandfather, and knew him as a very quiet, kind presence. "He never raised his voice. He had a powerful goodness." She grew up and wore her McCallie sweatshirt into a class at Furman University. A boy noticed it, and told her his father had graduated from McCallie. She told him she was Major Burns' granddaughter, "and he promptly called his father to tell him. When he spoke Granddaddy's name, his father began to cry."

Elliott Davenport was honored to be a pall-bearer at the ALB funeral. He remembers Maj. "patrolling the quadrangle in his grey suit and thin dark tie." Davenport says he "never knew a grandfather, but if I had, Maj. is the kind I would want."

Bud's family lived on Lookout Mountain, a ways away from campus. Grandson Graham and granddaughter Lucy tell their favorite family story of the children looking out the window and seeing Granddaddy coming up the driveway bearing packages of Cracker Jacks. Their mother Graham, who unlike the delighted children understood the distance he had come, always smiled at his opening line:

"I was just in the neighborhood on the way to get gasoline and thought I would stop by." (Lookout Mountain and his filling station were about 20 minutes apart.)

Graham appreciated the fact that in public Maj. introduced her as daughter, not daughter-in-law. "To be included with Helen was loving and accepting to me as Bud's wife."

Think about the wisdom of so doing, and it's linked to the French idiom. In the language that Maj. taught, there is no daughter-in-law but instead *belle-fille* or beautiful daughter. How much sweeter (and more accurate) is the French definition of this relationship. Maj. was Graham's *beau-père,* her beautiful father, not her father-in-law.

Grandson Graham caught this in saying that "Granddaddy was sweet and warm," then continued in the ever-present tense: "I love him very much." His mother agrees. "He was dear in his love and concern for the children. When one was sick he would call each day to follow up on how every child was doing. I love my grandchildren, but I don't do that!"

She continues, "Maj. was my claim to fame. Another fond memory was going out to McCallie basketball games and watching him speak to each boy, as if that person were the only person with whom he wanted to talk. With all the demands on his attention, to treat each person like that was remarkable. Everything he did was loving." There it is again, a powerful goodness.

Sunday dinners at the Burns home with the whole family often got interrupted by a phone call. Somebody needed him somewhere. He kept focused, however, on those grand grandchildren of his. An image survives of then-retired Maj., leaning against the chain-link fence by the McCallie Lake, watching a grandson at play at McCallie's Summer Camp.

Here's where the story takes a detour. Since 1905 the definitive prep school rivalry has been between Baylor School and McCallie. In the early 1970s boys had to be seven to attend McCallie's summer camp. Baylor, however, allowed five-year-olds, and so oldest grandson Lee at age five started his days on the Baylor campus! The family still has Lee's Baylor beanie.

That image may have been more than Maj. could bear. When next grandson Jim reached five, the rule somehow got changed and Jim was 100 percent McCallie, much later being elected to the McCallie Board of Trustees.

Their mother remembers a summer camp photograph of Maj. sitting beside grandson Lee. "I doubt most people who have seen this picture realize that the boy with Maj. is a grandson. It could be any McCallie camper in that photograph. That is how Maj. was with the boys, with each boy."

Being a school man almost always begins in the classroom. For Maj. it began with teaching English and Latin classes because only they were available in 1925. One might say the chief professional end would be becoming head of school. Not so for Maj. *Belle-fille* Graham believes that "Maj. would never have wanted to be head of McCallie. He was right where he wanted to be, as dean."

In that place, he could sit beside thousands, kin or no kin, so that you couldn't even tell the difference.

FAITH
to sight

As with the singing of the Alma Mater, vigorous on the last lines, Cliff Hudson has the same rich memory of Maj. leading the singing of "Love Lifted Me."

"Almost every week in chapel Major Burns led 'Love Lifted Me' with great gusto and vigor. If we were not responsive enough on the chorus, he would chide us and shame us into doing better. Just as the student body would put a loud and lusty exclamation point at the end of the Alma Mater, we would also get rowdy on the last three words and notes of the chorus: LOVE... LIFT-ED...ME!

"I carried this memory into my own ministry in the Cumberland Presbyterian Church. I have led this hymn countless time in worship and have always remembered Major Burns' rendition."

Maj. went to Memorial Hospital in late October of 1977 for surgery, necessitated by a diabetic ulcer in his foot. Memorial is directly on the path between Burns' childhood home and his home at McCallie. One night in the hospital, his pastor Dr. Ralph Mohney stopped by. He reported "a good visit, and then as I started to take his hand and offer a prayer he said, 'Before we pray, could we affirm our faith together in the words of the creed?' Together Maj. and I did so."

I believe in God, the Father Almighty,
maker of heaven and earth;
and in Jesus Christ his only Son, our Lord;
who was conceived by the Holy Spirit,
born of the Virgin Mary,
suffered under Pontius Pilate,
was crucified, dead, and buried;
the third day he rose from the dead;
he ascended into heaven,
and sitteth at the right hand
of God the Father Almighty;
from thence he shall come to judge
the quick and the dead.

I believe in the Holy Spirit,
the holy catholic church,
the communion of saints,
the forgiveness of sins,
the resurrection of the body,
and the life everlasting. Amen.

In the Bible ALB studied and lived, 2 Corinthians 5:7 declares that "we live by faith, not by sight." In 1 Corinthians 13:12 the apostle Paul describes the next step. "For now we see only a reflection as in a mirror; then we shall see face to face.

Now I know in part; then I shall know fully, even as I am fully known." After 75 faithful years Maj. was about to see fully, to know fully, the riches of heaven.

His death a week later on November 1, All Saints Day, was blamed on a blood clot in the lung. His body lay in state at the McCallie Chapel, as was part of his advance directive. Boys were honor guards for his body, and pallbearers. Rance Cleaveland was assigned a place beside the casket. "I remember my knees knocking as I took my turn standing in the chapel next to his casket, afraid I would have to sneeze or scratch or do something else to detract from the solemnity of the occasion. The things boys think about. . . . "

Two days later was the service at the First-Centenary United Methodist Church, the church he served for 35 years as a young adult Sunday school teacher and also as Administrative Board member. (How on earth did he find time for that?)

Jim Daughdrill Jr. thanked God for his friend, noting in his prayer that "few times do we see life so lived--not so much to get as to give; not so much to have, as to serve, and to teach and to love…our lives are richer because of Your goodness shown to us in his love--and yes, in his rebuke--but always his forgiveness and his strength and his faith."

The *Knoxville News-Sentinel* headline startled Tom Biggs, who put on paper what he would have said to Maj. "Is that any way for you to slip away? Lying, as I was, in a late-evening bed, thumbing the thick pages of a Wednesday newspaper, and across my eyes came: **ARTHUR BURNS DIES.**

"Now what (pray), pray tell, am I supposed to do with that? How (in God's name) can I be expected to handle that? After all you were--to me and all those others--to have no warning. What are my three years of memories supposed to do with that--and the article: 'Services will be tomorrow for Arthur Lee Burns, the Mr. Chips of the private McCallie School. Burns, associate headmaster of the exclusive boys' school, died yesterday at age 75. He joined the staff in 1925. His mandatory retirement five years ago slowed his activities, but he visited the school daily.'

"Is that your eulogy? Are my remembrances supposed to settle for those two paragraphs this November late evening?

"The least you could have done was shake me, or yell at me with that booming voice that could silence a rowdy Study Hall. Or you could have called my name out, like you did in chapel; and I could come trembling to that small office-inside-an-office and find you poring over a desk full of papers. You could look straight at me with those sad, Basset-hound eyes and tell me you'd had enough. I could handle that."

The news of Maj.'s death spread among his boys. Jim Talley said it was like losing a member of your family. Tom McCallie affirmed that "the Lord may now reveal to him the influence for good he exerted in the lives of many."

Andy Smith recalled that "Maj. had a presence and a bearing. And my goodness he had touch." Although stories can be told, as they have been on these pages, full of dialog, it was not so much what Maj. said as who he was. His presence. And his touch.

The threads of faith of this churchman, this hymn-lover, this humble Christ-follower are woven wordlessly and undeniably through each paragraph of the story of his life. Colleague Dick Smith recalled that one of Maj.'s favorite Bible verses was Micah 6:8. "And what does the Lord your God require of you but to do justice and to love mercy and to walk humbly in the sight of your God."

Requirements met, ALB.

Charles Stribling Jr., McCallie humor still intact, imagined his own entrance to heaven someday.

"This is my version of the afterlife.

"I'll be walking along, and a strand of 'gold line' (rappelling rope) will appear in front of me. I'll look up and see Houston Patterson, with helmet and Camel cigarette. He'll say, 'Strib, time to come up, tie yourself in.'

"I'll ascend to eternity, where I'll be greeted by Chalmers McIlwaine, with an academic program that will take an eternity to complete.

"El Schmidt will give me my wings, with a good shoulder rub.

"Miles McNiff will give me an essay to write.

"Keen Dean James will give me a piece of cake with butter on it.

"Yo Strang will give me a piece of candy, and say things get better every year.

"Dr. Park McCallie will look at me and say 'Stribling Jr.: I am amazed.'

"Dr. Spence will caution me that things up here can't be torn down.

"And lastly, Major Arthur Lee Burns will look at me, check my name off the list, and say 'Stribling, late as usual, but you got to the right place.'"

EPILOG
ALB Three

July 1, 2014:

Arthur Lee Burns III, known as Lee,

McCallie Class of 1987,

returns to Missionary Ridge.

With degrees from Dartmouth and Harvard,

he becomes the eighth headmaster of

The McCallie School.

LEE
in his own words

My earliest boyhood memories are of McCallie, and, like countless McCallie men, they somehow involve Major Burns, my grandfather.

I loved sports, and I loved my grandfather, and we shared many happy afternoons on the campus cheering on McCallie athletic teams together. On spring afternoons, we sat on the wooden blue bleachers down the third base line, ate pink cotton candy and rooted for the Big Blue baseball team. I wore my blue and white #44 basketball jersey into Davenport Gym as we cheered on the basketball teams of the early 1970s, especially that 1974 team.

At the end of my days of McCallie Day Camp, he came to meet me by the side of Davenport Gym. He'd give me a quarter to buy a drink, usually a grape Fanta, and, as I sat there with him before getting on the bus, he'd often tell me about McCallie, including many of its legendary teachers and administrators.

195

My favorite picture is one that Warren James '43 took of my grandfather and me one of those afternoons after camp. The drink machine was sold out of Fanta that day, so I'm drinking a Coke instead. I can see in his eyes in that picture his love for me. It was a love that he shared and gave to thousands of McCallie boys during their years.

He was my grandfather, but he was also a surrogate father to countless McCallie boys. I didn't realize that as a little boy, of course, but I've come to understand and appreciate that influence from the many, many times that McCallie alumni that have told me, or written to me, to tell what an important man he was to them. Often, these grown men begin crying when they talk about him, when they tell me Maj. stories--stories of toughness, yes, but always of love, too.

I am certain that my life's path and purpose has been largely shaped by him. I saw and learned of a man who made a difference in others, who gave of himself, who devoted himself, to help boys grow into men of honor, truth and duty. These boys needed him, and his investment in their lives gave him fulfillment and purpose and glorified the God he served.

Through him, I learned of McCallie, and I developed a deep love for McCallie. I developed a deep respect for the men and women who had devoted their lives to building the school, and building its boys into men. I saw the nobility of educators, and the nobility of McCallie.

196

McCallie alumni and even students today stand on the shoulders of men like my grandfather. Though he died when I was eight, and though that's been several decades, I am confident that I carry a piece of him and his spirit in me. And, I hope and think, he looks down on McCallie and has that same smile and pride in our school that he did in that picture in 1974.

ALB: 1902-1977

SCRIBE
student

Maj. welcomed me to the Class of 1957
as the third McCallie son of our family.

He comforted me
when my brother Guille and our father
died the following summer.

He taught me French.

He put his hand on my shoulder and
wordlessly turned me toward home
when I was suspended the next year.

He made sure I walked the bullring
the Sunday morning before graduation
for checking in late after the Final Dance.

I was as sure that I was his favorite
as I was that every boy felt the same.

He wrote a letter
about coming back to McCallie to teach,
speaking of this calling as
"Kin to the ministry, Boy. Kin to the ministry."
So I came.

At his retirement in 1972 and his death in 1977,
I wrote about him for the alumni magazine.

He was my excellent mentor.

HAH

SCRIBE
daughter

For the past 45 years a small scrap of paper
has accompanied me everywhere,
from adulthood to Texas to career to marriage
to Oregon and back home.

It came from the grace of my father's hand
one summer day--
the same hand that packed a sandwich
and an apple for me to take to work
and tucked the note
inside the brown paper bag.

On this paper always in my wallet
are written in blue ink four abiding words:

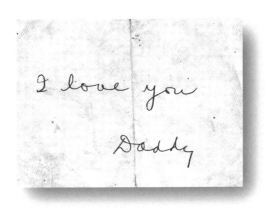

HBS

SCRIBE
storyteller

I married a man who keeps a photograph
of ALB beside the family photographs,
a man who still seeks to bear the imprint of ALB
in his behavior and character.

In October 1976 *The Chattanooga Times*
published a story
about the iconic Major Burns
of McCallie School.
The article bore my byline.
The story went and went,
filling an entire newspaper page.

And still the story goes on and on.

The Burns family carefully saved
every letter and document
concerning their patriarch.
(How did they know we would need them?)

The call for more ALB stories
went out to his boys, and scores responded
with razor-sharp memories
of a man who had been dead for 36 years.
We are their scribes, and this is their book.

We have passed it on.

JHH

ALB: Indelible influence indeed.

SOURCES

voices past and present

Wiley Adkins '56 Haddon Allen '66 Curtis Baggett '65 Michael Bailey Howard Baker '43 David Balloff '72 Steve Bartlett Charles Battle '60 Lloyd Baxter '44 Charlie Beard Roderick Beddow '44 Gary Beene '66 Irwin Belk '41 Bill Benoit '38 Wendell Berry Rob Betz '70 Tom Biggs '64 Frank Bird '40 Elliott Blaydes '45 & '46 E'Lane Bobo Mark Bode '69 Pete Branton '42 Mac Bridger '37 Jim Bruce '63 Bud Burns Jr. '55 Arthur Lee Burns III '87 Graham Smith Burns Graham Walker Burns May Burns Burke Hardwick Caldwell '40 Buck Camp '57 Howard Cannon '43 Henry Carrington '41 Louis Carter '57 Charles Castner '47 Rance Cleaveland '78 Joe Coffield '44 Jim Corn '43 Malcolm Colditz '53 Lew Conner '56 Fielder Cook '42 Horace Coward Lee Coward '58 Thorne Crosby '60 Tim Culvahouse '74 Jim Dade '70 Bobby Dann '72 Hal Daughdrill '73 Jim Daughdrill '52 Jim Daughdrill IV '05 Elliott Davenport '78 Joe Ben Davis '58 Bob Denton '59 Tom Divine '73 Bob Dobyns '44 Sam Dougherty '57 Rod Dreher

Tom Drew '68 Herbert P. Dunlap Bill Dunn '41
Dee Dunn '41 Jakie Dunn '46 Murdock Dunn '38
Tom Edwards '55 Tom Eichelberger '43 Breck
Ellison '42 George Farrell '63 John Ed Faucette
'50 Julian Ficklen '46 Bob Franklin '78 Lanham
Frazier '38 John Frist '63 Charlie Gaar '50 Mills
Gallivan '69 Cecil Garrett '42 Phil Gibbs '34
Dan Gilchrist '59 Ned Giles '64 James Gillespie
'43 Malcolm Gladwell Larry Gold '61 Ed Good
'63 Jim Greenwalt '63 L. H. Gross Gene
Gwaltney '74 Joe Harper '42 Ron Harr '72 Bob
Harris '44 Theo Harvey '40 Thomas Hayes '88
George Hazard '64 Nelson Head '64 Thomas
Hendrick '43 Ed Henegar '54 Lyman Hodge '46
John David Hopkins '55 Robert Hovis '37
Turner Howard '65 Cliff Hudson '72 Dean
Hudson Rob Huffaker '78 Terrell Huggins '41
Greg Hullender '77 W. O. E. A. Humphreys
Herman Hunter '53 Ed Hurley '73 Irwin Hyatt
'53 Warren James Sr. Warren James Jr. 43
Charles Jarrett '44 Dick Johnson '33 Tiger Jones
'58 Dick Koella '40 Frank Kollmansperger '45
Carl Kincaid '42 Bob Lambert '42 Hanes
Lancaster '42 Ted Lannom '68 Walt Layson '56
Winston Linam '44 Bill Lorino '57 Dooley
Lothrop '42 Ed Loughlin '79 Jim Lyle '49 Pogo
Maddox '63 Tom Makepeace '71 George
Marshall '70 George McCall '63 John McCall '61
Pete McCall '60 Franklin McCallie '58 J. Park
McCallie Jim McCallie '56 Spencer McCallie Sr.
Spencer McCallie Jr. '28 Spencer McCallie III '55
Tom McCallie '60 Dick McCubbin '45 Don
McGregor '78 Pancho McGregor '52 Chalmers
Moore Stirling McIlwaine '21 David McLain '59
Sandy McMillan '69 Doug Millar '41 Prentice
Miller David Milligan '57 Martha Smallwood

Milligan Jim Millis '41 Elise Mitchell Randy Mobley '67 Ralph Mohney Robert Moore '58 Sarah Moore Benji Morris '48 Buck Moseley '50 Barry Moser Maury Nicely '89 John Parham '58 Richard Park '55 Barry Parker '63 Houston Patterson '43 Gene Peek '34 Phinizy Percy '39 Osborne Perry '42 Buck Petry '72 David Phillips '67 Anne Pitts Robert Pritchett '63 J. B. Ramsey '41 Dan Rather '53 Susan Smartt Register Paul Renfroe '74 Craig Robinson Bill Rogers '51 Mark Rollinson '54 Lucy Burns Rose Preston Russell '59 Penny Sanders Buck Schimpf '67 Gene Schimpf '43 Nick Senter '39 Merrill Sexton '60 Ed Shackeroff '66 Jack Shannon '44 Alf Sharp '43 Sonny Sherrill '43 Martin Shofner '70 Harold Sibold '45 Bob Sims '42 Andy Smith '66 Audrey Smith Blackwell Smith '73 Mitzi Smith Richard I. Smith Robert Smitherman '40 Ed Snodgrass '73 Linda Snodgrass Jim Speake '63 Joe Stamper '65 Walt Stamper '41 Gerry Stephens '43 John Ed Stone '44 Larry Stone '75 Carol Burns Stoney Charles Stribling Sr. '42 Charles Stribling Jr. '71 Paul Swank '39 Hugo Taliaferro '42 Jay Talley '65 Jim Talley '42 Mitch Taylor '63 Rob Taylor '76 Sledge Taylor '70 Ronnie Thomas '66 David Thompson '65 Mark Thompson '43 John Varner Charles Vernon '43 John Vickers '43 David Walke '43 Bobby Walker '43 Bob Walker '58 Caroline Walker Kirk Walker '69 Mary McCallie Ware Hornsby Wasson '22 Ned Watts '55 Bill Weigel '56 Calvin Wells '42 Katherine Burns White Phil Whitley '58 Jack Wiener '78 Nick Wilkinson '96 Jimmy B. Williams '51 Pat Williams '40 Virginia Wrinkle Trent Zeppa '44

Telling Treasures Press,
creator of this book, encourages you
to recall the stories and values
that shaped you and to pass them forward
in conversations, in letters, in prayers,
and in enduring ink.

The font is Chatype. According to Steven Heller writing in *The Atlantic,* "Chattanooga, Tennessee has the distinction of being the first city in the United States to have its very own typeface. Designed by Chattanoogans Jeremy Dooley and Robbie deVilliers with support from fellow designers D.J. Trischler and Jonathan Mansfield, the … typeface was released on Oct. 31, 2013." Its shapes and proportions are influenced by the superstructure of Chattanooga's Walnut Street Bridge.

PHOTOGRAPHS provided and made by Helen Burns Sharp, Graham Walker Burns, Matt Brown, Warren James '43, Jim Daughdrill '52, George Hazard '64, & Ron Harr '72

The authors are thankful for help from Dr. Kirk Walker, Billy Faires, Penny Grant, Thomas Hayes, John McCall, Elise Mitchell, Sarah Moore, Joe Painter, Anne Pitts, Jeff Romero, Casey Rowland, Kenny Sholl, Audrey Smith, Mitzi Smith, & Caroline Walker.

Henry Alexander Henegar Jr.
henry.henegar@gmail.com
Jane Humphrey Henegar
janehenegar@gmail.com
Helen Burns Sharp
untiedlaces@gmail.com

NOW IT'S YOUR TURN

If you are young,
find someone to walk beside you,
to go before you to help you find your way.

If you are a generation beyond your youth,
fall into step beside someone younger
who travels on rough terrain.
Place your hand on the younger one's shoulder.

If you are growing old and looking back,
thank God for the ones who walked with you
when your steps were unsteady.

And remember you can walk this way still.

We learn to live well by watching someone else do it.
Your guide might be a shoulder's breath away,
or alive only in your memory,
or might come to life in the pages of a book.
This book, even.

To learn how, please see ALB.